EIGHT PATHS OF *Purpose*

TUVIA TELDON

outskirts press

Outskirts Press, Inc.
http://www.outskirtspress.com

Paperback ISBN: 978-1-9772-1580-2
Hardback ISBN: 978-1-9772-2264-0

Library of Congress Control Number: 2019911157

PRINTED IN BULGARIA

Table of Contents

FOREWORD
The Hat Maker

*W*hat happens when you thought you boarded the plane for Paris, but you land in Timbuktu?

Fifteen months after Chaya, my wonderful wife, and I were married in 1977, we were blessed with our first-born son. Our joy was boundless - until he was five hours old. Yes, that's *hours*. I will never forget the moment the resident walked into our Long Island hospital room and told us that our baby was born with a type of cystic fibrosis (CF) that would require emergency lifesaving surgery.

As far as we knew, there was no history of CF in either of our families. We were in total shock.

Following successful surgery, he spent a month in the hospital. We named him Boruch Nisan, which in Hebrew means he was a "blessed miracle," even though we were told that we should expect therapies, hospitalizations, and an ongoing decline in his health.

Soon after, the hospital geneticist told us there was a twenty-five percent chance that any future children born to us would have CF. To add insult to injury, we were then told Boruch's care would cost us about $50,000 a year.

We were beyond devastated.

Up to the day of his birth, we were secure that we had our basic purpose in life well defined. I had studied much to understand the teachings of Judaism and Kabalah[1], and we were looking forward to an exciting future together. But I became angry, and all I had were questions. How could this happen to us? What did we do to deserve this? What would happen to our marriage, our aspirations, and our future children? My entire sense of reality seemed to vanish in the face of shock. I refused to see any justification for such a turn of events in our young lives.

It took me more than a year to emotionally accept the fact that my son and his illness were part of our lives. I was not given a choice in the matter—only in how I would react to it. I could choose to be in victim mode or flow mode. To choose the latter, I would have to dig much deeper into myself and the wisdom of the sages. Except this time it was not for widening my knowledge base; it was for my spiritual and emotional survival.

Slowly I was able to see positive developments connected to my son's illness. The people we met because of him and the compassion we grew to have for people with special needs all gave deep meaning to his life. We came to see him as a typical child who happened to have CF. As his hospital friend Eli would later say, "I have CF, but CF doesn't have me." Our love for him grew, and we were happy parents, at peace with his condition and medical needs. He had a great personality and a captivating laugh. With time we found purpose in our new life. I accepted the fact that in my very public life I would be known as "the rabbi who has a kid with CF."

During the next eight years we were blessed with four healthy and wonderful boys, and Boruch's health was relatively stable. Life was wonderful.

---

1   The Kabalah is the spiritual branch of Judaism that was established with the writing of the Zohar by Rabbi Shimon bar Yochai (100 – 160 A.D.E.). It is the foundation upon which Chabad theology is based.

When Boruch turned nine, though, his health took a turn for the worse. His hospital stays increased. His precarious medical condition kept the whole family on a roller-coaster and dictated every day's schedule. We all watched as our son and brother slowly got sicker and sicker.

By the time he turned twelve, his condition was very serious. Fortunately, after many reviews and interviews, he was accepted into a new program to receive a double lung transplant at the Children's Hospital of St. Louis, just two blocks from my parents' home. He would be the first pediatric double-lung recipient in the country! We were thankful for this incredible opportunity to give him the gift of life, but we were also aware that it came with no guarantees.

Boruch's condition was very fragile, and we had no idea what this new venture would involve for all of us. Fortunately the transplant staff members guided us through step by step, as best they could. After a nerve-racking and precarious two-month wait, we received word just in the nick of time that a pair of matching lungs became available.

The operation was a success. My son and wife returned home to a well-publicized landing at the "Lung Island" Islip Airport three months after surgery, soon to be followed by his amazing bar mitzvah. We were ecstatic, and I frequently had to pinch myself to realize that my son was now a healthy little boy. His odyssey was covered closely by the Long Island newspaper, *Newsday*, and inspired thousands of people. We received letters from total strangers who were delighted about his recovery. We were overjoyed and felt blessed in many ways.

The unspeakable then happened. Boruch had a quick and massive rejection of his new lungs and it was all over.

My son was dead.

No words can describe the excruciating emotional and physical pain of our loss. I never knew that eyes could shed so many tears. No family or friends could heal our broken hearts. No person could console us. It felt like my entire body was paralyzed with grief and pain, like a poison pill had been released within me. The roller-coaster ride had come to the end. All those years, all the love and the struggle, and suddenly it was over, just like that.

I knew full well that I was totally unprepared to navigate myself and my family back to a healthy place. My challenge was to "stretch the bungee cord" so that my head and, more importantly, my heart could encompass not just life's normal events, but also the best and the worst of life. With small steps I slowly but surely got back on my feet. The birth of our daughter four months later, after five boys, brought much needed joy, and life, back into the house.

We were often asked "does your son's illness and death ever cause you to question God's existence?" My answer was very simple and straightforward. Either God exists or doesn't exist; it doesn't depend on my family. Either it took a Creator to bring this incredible world into being, or it created itself. I choose to believe that a Higher Power created it. With that said, I did have a choice to be angry, or to ignore this Creator. Or I could believe this Higher Power is removed from the world, and not involved in our lives. However, I did not want to embrace any of these mindsets.

My only real choice was to believe that God had some type of purpose for this, just as a doctor gives a painful shot to a crying youngster, and as a seed rots in the ground before it sprouts. My burning question was what purpose could this Higher Power possibly have for bringing such suffering into the world, and specifically to my family?

As a result, I was driven to search for answers about purpose, and hopefully find some meaning in all of this pain. I started writing this book during the seven-day mourning period in June 1991, and continued on and off as a labor of love and healing for twenty eight years.

In the beginning, putting my efforts into this book was my way of feeling connected to my deceased son. I spent much time crying - by myself, with Chaya, and with other parents who had lost children. As time went on, the book evolved beyond dealing with finding purpose in suffering, and I realized that its ideas could help many people better fulfill their specific purpose in life, whatever the circumstances may be. So I worked for years to reformulate these ideas so they can personally address people of all backgrounds, nationalities and religions (or lack thereof).

The thoughts in this book simply reflect my personal filter for the many teachings that are incorporated into my life, combined with many life lessons. Much of it is based on simple observations about life. I share it with you now in the hope that it will help you better fulfill your purpose in life, in many ways.

It is said that if one has a book inside his or her heart and mind, one has an obligation to write it. As Maya Angelou said, "There is no greater agony than bearing an untold story inside of you." This is the book that I had to write.

A great sage once commented, "When I teach, I am like a hat maker who fashions hats in many sizes. Whoever comes into my store can try them on, and if they find a hat that fits, so be it." I will try to be your hat maker. If some of the life tools you read about in this book fit you, I do hope that you will wear them. My experience and my heart tell me that acquiring these hats will help you face daily events with more meaning and purpose, and help elevate your journey through life.

INTRODUCTION
The Paradox of Purpose

*T*here is much healthy discussion today about the role that purpose should and does play in our lives. Millions of people of all ages are taking jobs based not just on salary, but also on the feeling that they are fulfilling a meaningful purpose through their work. Connecting to a meaningful purpose in life is a well-accepted goal to strive for.

Large and small corporations are making no secret of how social action is a high priority in their corporate identity next to profits, employee satisfaction, and security. An October 2016 article in *Harvard Business Review* states that "We hear more and more that organizations must have a 'purpose.' Purpose is on the agenda of the World Economic Forum in Davos and discussed by celebrity CEOs… Oxford University and Ernst and Young found that public dialogue on purpose has increased five-fold between 1995 and 2016." (1)

This trend is gaining momentum. The business world is focusing on purpose-driven companies for increased employee retention and profits.[2] But outside of the business world I have seen very few studies that strive to truly understand the nature of purpose, and the impact it has on our lives and on society at large. Not enough is written that explores how the phenomenon of purpose actually works and especially not about how it thinks!

---

2   For instance see https://www.forbes.com/sites/rodgerdeanduncan/2018/09/11/

Why is it important to know how purpose "thinks?" What does that even mean? Simply put, if there is a method of understanding purpose, it is important to familiarize ourselves with it. If we want to fulfill a purpose, we should have some idea of how to be in sync with how purpose functions.

I am not referring to the specifics of whatever we may decide to do to fulfill a purpose, whether it be saving the whales or donating to a local charity or self-actualization or raising an autistic child. What I mean is that it is important to know how best to align ourselves properly to our very own unique purpose. That is what "getting to know how purpose thinks" is all about.

Did you ever stop to think how we can connect to our purpose in a very real way? Is there a difference between a goal and a purpose, or between a meaningful life and a purposeful life, or between fulfilling "a" purpose and fulfilling "my" purpose? How do I know where to look for purpose? Who can I trust, and how do I stay on target? Why is it sometimes so hard to fulfill a purpose?

"Purpose" needs more of an expanded discussion. It needs some brave thinking that delves into the topic with a refreshing perspective. It needs a book with fresh ideas.

Eight Paths of Purpose is an introduction to this exciting topic. It discusses the "operating system" that drives a sense of purpose and encourages the reader to decide how to apply it.

Whatever your nationality, belief system, or political leanings may be, whether you believe in a Higher Power or not, the tools provided in this book will help you fulfill your purpose to a greater degree. It does not try to define your individual purpose as other books about purpose may; it simply provides the general overview of how purpose thinks, so you can better sync with your core purpose and then explore its many applications.

> *It's not enough to have lived. We should*
> *be determined to live for something.*
> —WINSTON CHURCHILL

The topic of purpose is potentially controversial and difficult to describe. There are so many varied ways by which people all over the world connect to and practice their purpose.

Some may say that once you have financial security and after your children are either out of the house or independent, there is no other valid purpose other than having fun and enjoying yourself.

Nevertheless, billions of people now and throughout history have aspired to fulfill many purposes in life. Health professionals, teachers, police officers, clergy, military, and social workers, believe they are fulfilling a meaningful purpose serving others or serving a greater cause. Many people find great purpose in religion, politics, family, jobs, hobbies, giving to charity, volunteering, or other endeavors.

Are they all deceiving themselves about fulfilling a purpose as a result of some human weakness, or are they really connecting to something very deep within themselves?

Where do we take this conversation to answer this question and explore what "purpose" means?

Let's begin by reviewing our lessons from high school science. Didn't we all learn that every atom, molecule and cell in the universe fulfills its purpose naturally? The bee and the flower of course don't understand why they do what they do, but they fulfill their purpose nevertheless. Every drop of water in the ocean, the chemicals in the ground, a fox in the forest, bacteria in the air, organs in our body, and stars in the sky are fulfilling their purpose naturally and in harmony.

The complexities of nature—biology, chemistry, physics, astronomy, geology, and meteorology—are all programmed to do their jobs in producing this phenomenon we call our universe. If any of the major laws of physics were changed by even one-tenth of one percent, the universe would not exist as we know it. Even the destructive forces of nature are part of this perfect balance.

Yes, this is all true. Everything does behave in a predictable way to fulfill its individual purpose—except us.

What a paradox; humans, with our superior intellect, are the only ones in this vast universe who do not naturally fulfill a purpose.

In fact, the crown of creation seems to be destined to play a guessing game whether we have any purpose at all.

Something in this scenario does not make sense!

It seems as if there is some built-in mechanism that deliberately stands in our path and blocks our ability to fulfill our purpose. This is the paradox of purpose.

Many of us feel that we are wandering through life like a ship without a rudder or a ball in a pinball machine that is bounced around from one event to another, trying to make sense of life on a day-to-day basis. Life seems to place obstacles in our path deliberately, making it hard to remain positive as we grow, and it can get more complex with time. A deep belief in God doesn't protect us from this roller coaster, as Chaya and I found out with the birth of our first-born son.

The person without a purpose is like
a ship without a rudder.
—Thomas Carlyle

Some people may avoid any pursuit of purpose because they see that history is filled with arrogant dictators or demagogues who used purpose as a rationale for committing horrific acts against humanity. We don't want to be like them.

We may therefore train ourselves to inhibit any feeling of, or desire for, fulfilling a purpose in life. We may be afraid to trust our instincts out of fear of appearing foolish or becoming vulnerable.

It's no wonder that many people believe that life is no more than just a series of unrelated, accidental events. They have given up on finding a purpose in their lives and the events that fill them. They are easily overwhelmed by what they see, read, and hear. The maze seems just too complex to navigate.

On the other hand, I also see that many people look with admiration upon others who are driven by a purpose, feeling that those people have a key to the secret of a happy life that they may be missing.

It's always inspiring to me to meet people
who feel that they can make a difference in
the world. That's their motive, that's their
passion.... I think that's what makes your
life meaningful, that's what fills your own
heart, and that's what gives you purpose.
—Maria Shriver

In fact a September 2013 Pew Research Center survey shows that "a large majority of all respondents 'strongly disagreed' (56%) or 'disagreed' (36%) that life does *not* serve a purpose, with *only* 3% saying they agreed or strongly agreed." (2)

My concern is about the millions or billions of people who sense or believe there is a purpose but don't know what to do about it. Perhaps they really do want to feel and/or strengthen their sense of purpose, but they inhibit a sense of purpose because they don't know where to turn or who to speak to. Nothing they have heard, read, or seen about the subject of purpose really speaks to them. They need some new tools to connect to their sense of purpose.

> *If you can tune into your purpose and really align with it, setting goals so that your vision is an expression of that purpose, then life flows much more easily.*
> —Jack Canfield

So we see that purpose seems to be enveloped in mystery.

The truth is that we will never be able to fully understand the real purpose of our lives or the reason why things happens to us, but surely if we can put a man on the moon and figure out the DNA map of the human body, we can make significant headway to unravel this mystery as well.

At the least, there must be some type of 'DNA of purpose' that applies to all of humanity—a "purpose operating system" that transcends nationality, race and religion, one that connects us to the core of the human experience and helps us better fulfill our inherent purpose.

To attempt to understand and develop this dimension in our lives, we need some healthy, grounded guidelines. We need to learn how this curious phenomenon of purpose works, how it is connected to our inner being, and how it can help us all have a more fulfilling life.

I think most of us would indeed like to know about a safe and traveled path to make our life more purposeful. If we could feel a core purpose in our guts, then we could trust it and enjoy the journey. This is what *Eight Paths of Purpose* aims to achieve. Sit back and enjoy the ride.

The order in which the eight paths are described in the book does not constitute a particular order for living a life of purpose. Each individual can adapt their purpose path(s) in a manner that fits them, as we will discuss in chapter 6.

At the end of each of the first four chapters I will list the 'purpose paths' discussed to that point, highlighting those discussed in that chapter in bold.

Life can be an ongoing process of discovering our unique purpose and learning how to be true to that purpose. It is accomplished by illuminating our surroundings with this purpose and constantly growing in our pursuit of it.

PART I
How Purpose Thinks

CHAPTER ONE
Changing the World

*F*rom the beginning of time great people have aspired to fulfill a great purpose in life.

Politicians campaign to change society.

Poets create inspiring descriptions of life and lofty goals to reach.

Scientists aspire to unleash the great potential that lies hidden in the simplicity of nature.

Spiritual giants teach about the greatness of revealing our hidden soul power.

Despots force their purposes on others, often causing great pain and suffering.

For many of us, fulfilling a lofty purpose in life seems to be an activity reserved for the privileged few—those that have money, intellect, talent, and/or grit. Contemporary culture has influenced some people to believe that fame, fortune, and power infuse life with purpose. The rest of us seem to be happy to stay healthy, pay the bills, and enjoy our family, without the perks and risks of aspiring to fulfill some non-definable purpose.

Efforts and courage are not enough
without purpose and direction.
—PRESIDENT JOHN F. KENNEDY

What happens though when we give a little different definition to the word *purpose*? What if it doesn't have to be located at the top of some mountain? What if it is sitting on our kitchen table, in our bedroom, on our tongue, and in our wallets? What if we could see it in our family, in our coworkers, or in our daily challenges?

We tend to minimize the great purpose found in little unseen acts, the quiet "ordinary" life that most of us live.

Let's redefine purpose so it can help us in our day to day choices and assist us in making our relationships, marriage, and family more complete. If only we could view purpose as a good friend which can keep us focused through life's ups and downs and catch us before we make the common mistakes we are all vulnerable to make.

If we choose so, our purpose can be like the air we breathe. It's always there ready for us to inhale whenever we want, sometimes consciously, sometimes unconsciously. It won't push its way in, but it is always available.

When purpose comes down to earth like this, its new identity looks much more attractive. It becomes an organic, holistic friend that can uplift even the simple and mundane activities that fill our day at work or at home. If you see your life in part as a journey, purpose provides lots of fuel.

I sense that when people feel they are doing something for a purpose, their energy level is often raised and they seem better prepared to overcome obstacles they may encounter.

Many of us try to connect to a purpose daily through fulfilling our potential at work and at home. I see around me how people believe in themselves enough to rise with—and above—the challenges of life. They inherently have the ability to turn a negative into a positive, the desire to make their lives better, and the drive to overcome obstacles. They try their best to transform a tragedy into something good, even if in only some small way. Just look at all the foundations and charities established by families who experienced loss.

Lillian lost her daughter in a car crash, and a few years later, on the same day, her husband passed away shoveling snow. She could have easily given up, but instead established COPE Foundation (Connecting Our Paths Eternally) to help hundreds of other grieving families.

Let's examine a few common approaches to living a life of purpose.

Many people try to fulfill a purpose in life by engaging in various types of meaningful activities or causes. This is very praiseworthy, and can lead to a fulfilling life, however one can be filling their time with meaningful activities (volunteering for great organizations) while avoiding the fulfillment of pressing, but unenjoyable, responsibilities, which are part of our real purpose.

Aren't we fulfilling an important purpose even when we care for frail parents or a special needs child, though we may not feel any meaning or fulfillment in this at all? Fulfilling our purpose does not always have to come in a package we enjoy or benefit from. Facing life's many tests and challenges may not feel meaningful at the time, but nevertheless they can be important for fulfilling our unique purpose.

Very often the terms meaningful and purposeful are used interchangeably, but it is important to note that there is a fine line between them. A meaningful life can be attained by doing many meaningful acts. However, a life of purpose is very focused on uncovering your specific purpose from within, and discovering why you are who you are, or why you are going through what you are going through.

Another common approach to purpose which is espoused in so many self-help books, psychological journals, and coaching tips, advises us to fulfill our purpose by putting our energies into acts of self-actualization or self-development.

"Develop your hidden potential." "Be happy against the odds." "Keep a positive attitude." "Overcome your obstacles." These are all lofty and important goals in life.

Developing our potential and reaching for the stars to make sure that we become all that we can become can surely be a praiseworthy accomplishment, but it can also be a great distraction from fulfilling our purpose. Living a life of purpose is not always accomplished through self-actualization[3]. This should be one tool in enabling us to fulfill our greater purpose. It is an important means to a greater end. But it does not make sense that this should be the ultimate goal of fulfilling a purpose in life. Life by definition is more multi-dimensional than that.

---

3   For more on this important topic see #5 of Purpose Pointers in chapter 5.

*True happiness ... is not attained
through self-gratification, but through
fidelity to a worthy purpose.*
—HELEN KELLER

Choosing any of the above-mentioned endeavors is admirable, but often there is a bit of guesswork involved in these choices. Until we understand how purpose thinks, we can't really be sure that we are choosing 'our' unique purpose.

The fact is that we have many choices that can make our lives better; however, the choices this book deals with are not limited to choices of good or bad, right or wrong, comfortable or uncomfortable. The *Eight Paths of Purpose* is focused on the daily choices we have to see purpose in our life or not to see purpose in our life.

This is an area of life that most of us are unfamiliar with and unprepared for. You may ask, "How are we supposed to see choices of purpose daily? What does that even mean?"

To answer this question, we have to understand the center of the purpose circle, the point from which all spokes of the purpose wheel originate. We have to understand the very core—the "DNA"—of purpose; purpose as it is wired deep in the human psyche. This DNA of purpose contains the script for how purpose thinks and how it works in our lives.

Just as every part of the universe has a purpose, so do people, just in a different way. Our purpose doesn't necessarily come naturally to us the way it does for the rest of the universe, but we do need to know the general parameters of this DNA.

As humans we sometimes have to choose in order to connect to our

DNA of purpose. We cannot wake up one day and decide that our purpose is to watch butterflies or play checkers all day and pass those things off as fulfilling our purpose.

Our first step is to look at the topic of purpose from a different angle.

Many people, when asked about a general purpose in life for all of humanity, wonder about some new idea or approach. "Let's try something unique that will inspire the masses or pique our curiosity to try to reach new heights." They question what new vistas can be conquered to fulfill some great purpose; how each of us to rise to the challenge of life.

However, when we are looking to understand the "operating system of purpose", or how purpose thinks, that question is the wrong one. In fact, perhaps we need not ask any questions at all. We don't need to come up with some creative or original formula of purpose. We just need to analyze our past.

The purpose is programmed within us, and we have been fulfilling it in a myriad of ways.

Indeed, we can all see a universal purpose in action by observing how billions of people, across the spectrum, feel they are fulfilling a meaningful purpose daily. We are programmed with a core purpose we feel is part of our inner identity. It is so clear that we can just extrapolate truth from the unquestionable reality around and within us.

Simply put, the purpose mankind has fulfilled over the millennium, and in particular over the past three hundred years, reveals for us the answer to our question. The choices humanity has made throughout history have helped societies accomplish tremendous feats over the centuries and fulfill an incredible purpose.

We consistently see that there is a human drive anchored deep within each of us that has fueled our ability to proactively transform much of the world around us.

As a result of hundreds of years of progress[4], we have harnessed the power of the atom, transformed sunlight into energy, and multiplied food production a thousand fold, all to make our world a better place to live in. The drive to fine-tune the raw materials at our disposal and elevate our living conditions has led to more than seven million patents just in the USA.

In industry we have turned the resources around us into tools for making the world a better place and our lives safer, easier, and more fulfilling.

> *Fact: Home appliances have reduced the average amount of work in the house from an average of sixty hours a week to fifteen hours a week.(3)*

We have used medical science to improve the quality of life, to eradicate many devastating diseases, to lessen pain, and to extend life. We transplant organs and operate on fetuses in utero.

> *Fact: Three hundred years ago the expected life span was forty, and one-third of children died by the age of five. Today our life span is seventy plus, and fewer than 6% of children in poor countries die before the age of five.*

In social issues we have improved lives and provided opportunities for personal and financial growth. Laws are continually passed to protect

---

4   Even before the Industrial Revolution, mankind was "fixing" the imperfections of the world, but at a much slower pace. Progress was being made but people were so absorbed with survival under 'governments' that often were so repressive, they were not able to fully develop this sense of purpose. The 1700s saw a two-fold explosion of democratic movements and scientific creativity, allowing people the freedom to pursue their purpose with greater intensity.

the environment, the rights of individuals, and even of animals.

> *Fact: Before the seventeen century, only 15% of Europeans could read and write. Today 90% of the world population under twenty-five can read and write.*

Wars have become an unpopular way of resolving conflicts. We have torn down the Iron Curtain and the Berlin Wall, and despots are being held accountable for their deeds. When disaster strikes nations rally to help, and countries have been saved from famine through the efforts of the world community.

> *Fact: Two hundred years ago the chances of dying in a war were 22/100,000 people, while today they are 1.2/100,000. Thirty years ago there were twenty-three wars in progress, and today there are only twelve. In 1988 there were 60,780 nuclear weapons. Today there are fewer than 10,000.*

Democracies have proliferated throughout the world, allowing more and more people the freedom to develop their potential.

> *Fact: Some 250 years ago democracies did not exist. Today almost two-thirds of the world population lives under democratically elected governments.*

Scientific research, the computer and the Internet have revolutionized global access to knowledge and communication, transforming international awareness that we are all part of a world community enabled to help each other.

> *Fact: Two hundred years ago, 90% of the world population lived in extreme poverty. In 2017 it was 10%.*

Some people call this simple progress, or part of the evolutionary process, but this does not explain the driving force behind these changes.

What is it that motivates us to explore the unknown and push the envelope in so many fields? Why do millions of us aspire to a job that connects us to this sense of purpose, whether as CEO of a tech firm, a salesperson for a construction company, a public servant, a nurse, or a teacher? How do we explain a 2018 survey of 2,285 workers across 26 industries, in which 9 out of 10 career professionals told researchers they would "sacrifice 23 percent of future earnings —an average of $21,000 a year—for work that is always meaningful"? (4)

Many large and small companies are working toward becoming purpose-driven companies, and many employees are looking to work in an environment that recognizes a core purpose of making the world a better place for all to live in. A recent Harvard Business Review article states that "in our consulting work with hundreds of organizations and in our research–which includes extensive interviews with dozens of leaders and the development of a theoretical model–we have come to see that when an authentic purpose permeates business strategy and decision making, the personal good and the collective good become one. Positive peer pressure kicks in, and employees are reenergized. Collaboration increases, learning accelerates, and performance climbs." (5)

Fortune magazine now has a special edition listing the top fifty companies that make "changing the world for the good" a part of their mission.

Jeffrey was a driven young man looking for a job in Austin in bio-engineering. He didn't want to be just like his dad and go after whatever job offered the highest salary. He was willing to sacrifice some income in order to work for a company that represented his values and accomplished something good for the world. Finally his choices came down to two jobs, both fitting the bill. He was ready to choose his number one, when he found on a quick search that the other was listed in the new *Fortune* magazine's "change the world" listing of corporations that "make social benefit part of their core business." That information convinced him that he would feel a stronger sense of purpose in his day-to-day work at company number two.

We feel fortunate to be making a positive difference in other people's lives and the world at large, even if it is in some small way. The will to be positive, to build, to invent, and overcome obstacles inspires most of us.

Our world is making this purpose more and more of a priority; so much so that it is clearer than ever that the motivation for fulfilling this purpose is truly ingrained in the human fabric.

Society at large is fulfilling a universal sense of purpose to improve and if possible fix the imperfections of our world.

This drive is an expression of something that comes from the core of who we are as human beings. We are wired, to varying degrees, to want to fulfill this purpose in our lives. It is not just self-actualization that drives these efforts. It is an inner desire to connect us to a greater purpose in life, to something greater than ourselves.

This "operating system" for how purpose thinks is the source for the great variety of purposes people engage in. Whether we feel our purpose is to fix up our house, aid survivors of a disaster, or become a college professor, a core DNA is driving us.

This also explains why it feels good inside to help another person, find a solution to a problem, or fix something that is broken. This "DNA of purpose" provides the drive for many people who want to be part of a cause bigger than they are. Some, as in the military, will even give their life for that cause. This is why we do things for the benefit of people we don't even know. We feel in a deep way that we are doing our small piece to make the world a better place.

Where did this core sense of purpose come from? What makes humankind the only species on earth that has the ability and willpower to improve its life and its future—to change itself and its environment? What is the DNA that fuels this age-old motivation?

Capitalism did not give birth to the drive to make the world a better place. It simply tapped into it to help us attain material success in life. Democracy allows us to pursue it and provides the environment for it to flourish. Human intelligence devises ways to reach our goals but doesn't provide the driving force. The world religions encourage it but did not create it.[5]

It is a universal purpose that is greater than any one source, any one religion, or any one philosophy. It requires no outside sages to verify it, because it is felt within every one of us. It is shocking in its simplicity. It is the quest to accomplish something meaningful in our personal lives and in the world at large. It is implanted deep in our psyche, our hearts, and our souls. It provides the fuel that drives humanity to try to fix this imperfect world.

We are internally wired to aspire to make the world a better place for

---

5   This approach to understanding the purpose of mankind was first expounded by the Jewish sages, based on Genesis 2:3, more than 3,300 years ago. In fact all branches of Judaism accept it as the universal purpose for all mankind, called *tikun olam b'malchus Shad-da*i in Hebrew, or "fixing the world according to God's sovereignty." This book explores the basis of *tikun olam* and eight applications of it in our lives.

ourselves and our children. Every time we take a step along this path, we feel an inner sense of accomplishment. Even if we have but a very small part in this process, we feel connected to the larger goal.

This internal wiring explains why so many people desire and enjoy contributing to make the world a better place. It is not just because they are selfless, beneficent, and giving individuals. It is also because they are in touch with, and driven by, a core human value.

Why else would Bill Gates, Warren Buffet, and 202 (as of 2019) of the most successful businesspeople in the world (from twenty-three countries) pledge to donate anywhere from 50% to 99% of their wealth? (6) I propose that it is not simply because they are wonderful and charitable people. Rather they truly feel in their bones that with this act they are fulfilling the greatest purpose their lives could possibly serve to significantly make the world a better place for future generations .

As Gates writes on his website, "We are inspired by the example set by millions of people who give generously (and often at great personal sacrifice) to make the world a better place."

C. Dean Metropoulos, a Greek-American investor and businessman who is one of the donors along with Gates, writes in his commitment letter, "I am proud more about our family's sense of goodwill, compassion, and love than of wealth building. The latter is exciting and challenging, but without the desire to help or try to make a difference in the lives of those far less fortunate, there is an emptiness of 'purpose' in more wealth and material possessions. One who cannot 'feel' this sense of purpose will truly arrive at the end of this life's journey quite empty."

This DNA does not dictate what lifestyle, cause, belief system, or philosophy to follow. It does not control us. It does not answer our questions about life. When we are aware of it, however, it does provide the "operating system" for us to know which inner voice we should listen to, and what our life goals should be built on.

It does help us think about our purpose in a healthy and productive manner. It whispers to us to help make choices in line with our core wiring. In fact, choices that are consistent with this operating system can be made with the confidence that they will lead to a greater sense of inner peace.

I propose to you that the desire to have a purpose and make the world a better place is cross-cultural,[6] although it is not based on culture or on learned behavior. We don't simply decide to make a difference in the world. We feel it in our bones that this is part of our core identity.

On what basis do I make a claim that this purpose is embedded in every human being? The answer is simple. Do you know any parents who do not feel that they would like to do something to make the world a better place for their children, grandchildren, or future generations? Even if they never act on that feeling due to oppression, survival issues, health or simple laziness, the fact that they even have such thoughts and/or dreams is because of their core sense of purpose.

Even those who do not have a family or are totally satisfied with life naturally want the world at large to get better. Even people with evil intent may believe in their sick way that their goal is to make the world a better place.

Every human is wired, to varying degrees, with this core purpose. For many it is a very active force in their lives. For others it is passive. For some people, for a variety of reasons, it can remain dormant until something happens in their lives or they are suddenly

6   For instance, in Japanese culture it is known as Ikigai.

motivated or they grow to a point where they want to engage in some type of purpose-oriented activity.

> Janette grew up in an underprivileged area of Pretoria. She never imagined that life could have a purpose, as her environment stifled any thoughts of personal growth, but from the Internet she knew there were other ways to live, and she dreamed about getting there. Through a series of events a tourist took a liking to her and helped her enroll in a college. She thrived in her academics and could have chosen many paths but was always drawn to the nonprofit field of work. She had discovered about herself that in her heart of hearts she wanted to do something to make the world a better place.

What better proof do we need to verify the existence of our "DNA of Purpose" than the fact that people with good health, loving families and many accomplishments, who may feel their life is purposeless, can easily lose the will to live. Often people feel a deep emptiness when they are out of touch with this inner wiring.

> Jin was a retired and aging bookkeeper living more than one hundred miles from her family in Tokyo. She had a productive life filled with activity, but she felt lonely and empty. As much as her family tried to lift her spirits, nothing seemed to work, and then a friend who practiced *Ikigai* invited her to volunteer at the local convalescent home. Once she did, she finally felt that her life had some purpose. Even though she worked there only twice a week, she became a happy woman.

Even those who happily live on automatic pilot and are not interested in trying to figure out the meaning of their everyday existential struggle, may still benefit from being part of a process which creates meaning in their lives. The mail clerk in an environmental law firm is part of the total effort producing a small change in the world. A janitor in a military hospital is still making a contribution to the total army effort. A single mom is struggling to do everything possible to provide a great upbringing for her two children. They are all connecting to their inner purpose on some level.

We should not take this core purpose for granted. We are the only members of the universe who are wired with this drive, each to a different degree. No other animate or inanimate matter has any purpose other than to be exactly what it is—nothing more and nothing less.

A kangaroo is not able to improve itself or even think about making a better life for future generations of kangaroos. Even the most advanced primates, or the smartest dolphins, do not try to make life better for future generations. They all have the luxury of fulfilling their purpose by doing exactly what they are programmed to do, but they can't intentionally change or break through their limitations. They don't have to deal with the paradox of purpose.

We alone have this amazing gift of purpose which makes each of us so unique in the universe, and we alone have to overcome the paradox of purpose by choosing to fulfill our purpose.

This core purpose should not be viewed as just an extra-curricular activity or a passing fad. It is the inheritance of every human being, rich or poor, healthy or sick, free or imprisoned. Through it we collectively work to elevate our lives and all of society, sometimes at great cost, with tremendous sacrifice, and by overcoming significant obstacles.

"Making the world a better place" is the core DNA and the operating system from which all eight paths of purpose develop. This is the center of the eight spoked wheel of purpose.

The eight paths are all *observable applications* through which people of different backgrounds, cultures and nationalities choose to direct and express their unique DNA of purpose.

We see in fact that many individuals follow this DNA of purpose in their professions, their passions, their charity, and/or their politics. Whether they do research to find solutions to real human challenges or they join the League of Women Voters to help in elections, the motivation may often be connected to this core purpose. It is a calling that many people aspire to pursue at some point in their lives.

As a result, I also count *'making the world a better place'* as **the first spoke of the eight purpose paths.**

Because of the efforts of these people and millions of others over the centuries, many of life's great challenges have been met. So much so that the drive to improve life today and in the future has taken on a whole new meaning and the potential is boundless.

The great accomplishments humanity has achieved have transformed our world over the years, but this makes up only one spoke in the Purpose Wheel.

With all said and done, the world is still far from perfect; conflicts and hatred still abound; imperfect, negative, and even evil choices by individuals and governments are still being made; injustice and pain are found everywhere; and new challenges we never dreamed of are being created daily. Many people still use the excuse of some "purpose" to kill and maim.

There is still much more to improve upon and accomplish in our world, so the challenge we must face now and every day is how to translate this purpose into our daily lives in a positive and practical way that we can trust, so we can make our unique contribution to creating a better future.

For that, we have to take our understanding of purpose to the next level and try to understand the importance of the other seven paths.

PURPOSE PATH

MAKE THE WORLD A BETTER PLACE

CHAPTER TWO
To Everything a Purpose

Is it difficult for you to imagine that you can have a unique role and purpose in making this world and your immediate environs a better place to live? It is not always easy to look at ourselves in the mirror and think that we do have the ability to identify those aspects of our life that need improvement, healing, or fixing, and make our unique contribution to the betterment of the world at large.

Would you feel you made a real difference in your life if you could "change the world for the better"? If so, you are not alone. A quick Google search on this theme comes up with over 8 million links. If you thought even once in your life that you could make the world a better place, it was probably not about benefitting just yourself, but also for the sake of your descendants and the rest of the world.

This is not our ego speaking; it is our unabashed belief in our worth as human beings.

The purpose of life is ... to be useful, to be honorable, to be compassionate, to have it make some difference that you have lived and lived well.
—RALPH WALDO EMERSON

Each one of us is a vital piece of a greater puzzle. Each of us is indispensable in some way and can make a unique contribution to the world that nobody else can. As Simon Jacobson wrote in *Towards a Meaningful Life*, "Birth is God saying you matter." (7) The world would not be the same without you!

In a life of purpose, the circumstances of our life set the stage upon which we strive to better ourselves and the world around us. We have a very organic relationship with our surroundings, which present us with the imperfections of life in need of improvement. We are uniquely positioned to meet their challenge and fulfill a purpose by improving these circumstances of our life.

No two people have the same combination of raw material—the same personality, reactions, talents, handicaps, and experiences. Surely nobody experiences life and its varied circumstances in the exact way we do, and nobody can fix the circumstances of our life the way we can.

By exerting our time, energy, and resources to improve our day-to-day environment, we are truly fulfilling our unique role in making our family and community a better place.

This is the second path of purpose. It is a direct outgrowth of the first path, but involves a whole different set of applications, to make positive changes for our family, community, and surroundings. It is the meat and potatoes of fulfilling a purpose, when we make whatever effort we can to make our life and the lives of others around us better in any myriad of ways. It is dealing with the micro, not the macro.

These first two paths are the inheritance of every human being. Fulfilling this individual purpose in life is not dependent on IQ, race, or creed. It is not limited to accomplishing some great feat or reaching a lofty goal. Purpose in life should be felt on Main Street and in our kitchen, just as much as in a place of worship, in the halls of Washington, or during an inspiring personal experience.

At one moment purpose may be expressed through our attendance at a PTA meeting; at another moment, how we handle a difficult situation at work or fix a broken appliance at home; at yet another it could be our decision to donate to an environmental cause in South America.

Collectively, if we all make an attempt to improve upon those circumstances of our lives which we feel we can positively affect, the world would be a much better place to live in.

These two paths complement each other, and many of us make efforts to work in both the macro and the micro simultaneously.

To continue our exploration of the paths of purpose, we need to understand how having a purpose in life is not the same as having a goal in life. In reality a life of purpose can be made up of many goals.

The goals help us fulfill our purpose, and the purpose can provide us with the overall drive to fulfill the goals. Every step of our journey is a crucial part of the purpose, and goals help us take those steps.

It is a great feeling to work toward and reach a goal, but that's not the whole purpose. The purpose is much larger than a goal, and lives on long after a goal is forgotten.

Take for instance our drive to procreate. According to basic biological principles, procreation is our main purpose as human beings. We need to keep the species alive. Adoption is another way to accomplish this.

Most of us, especially after we have children, don't view this as simply a goal in life. We see it as part of our essential purpose. As a result, everything we do to support and raise our children helps us fulfill this purpose. In fact, we may set and reach many goals during the course of fulfilling this purpose. Many of these goals will likely be in sync with our overall purpose to insure that our children will have an even better life than we do.

The drive to survive is another example of a way we are all fulfilling a purpose. Survival is not just a goal. It is something so deep within us it is unquestionably part of our essential purpose. This purpose can motivate people to work hard to make a living or alternatively to steal and deceive. It can motivate nations to great achievements or alternatively lead to war.

Today many of us don't have to think about pursuing this purpose in life; that is, until we have to. Survival surfaces as a purpose when we face a dangerous crisis, natural disaster, threat, tragedy, or thoughts of suicide. After 9/11 many of us felt strangely connected to this purpose in life, and realized how fragile we really are. In addition, during our lives we invariably face serious personal health issues with ourselves or another family member. At such times our mindset changes, and survival becomes a powerful force, very often driven by a sense that we must live.

For millions of people living in modern countries, and billions in many third world countries, this purpose is a real part of their daily lives and activities.

Having financial security is another aspect of the purpose to survive. We get a job and strive to have a sense of security because it is part of our core identity. We may have financial goals, and our income helps us reach some of those goals, but financial security is not just a goal. It is part of our core purpose to ensure that we and our family have food to eat and a roof over our heads.

Sometimes we don't really think of our job as being part of our purpose until we are faced with unemployment or financial insecurity. We then realize how essential our job is to our core being.

During a lifetime we set many goals in order to fulfill this purpose. Some are short-term and some are long-term, but undoubtedly all of them are for the purpose of keeping ourselves and our loved ones healthy and financially secure, so that we can aspire to accomplish an even greater purpose in life.

The drives to procreate and survive are **the third and fourth paths of purpose.**

The first four paths are general paths which can consume much of our lives. For many people inserting a sense of purpose in these paths can add great meaning to life, and enhance the feelings of success that we aim to achieve. Perhaps we are involved in the first two paths to some degree; perhaps happily raising (or already raised, or don't have) a family, and hopefully not dealing with health or other survival issues. Perhaps life's 'normal' challenges are pretty much under control, and do not weigh us down heavily. Perhaps we are relatively happy about our past and present successes, both personally and professionally.

It is important to note that even though we may be involved with any of these four paths, we may still need to mentally and emotionally align our efforts with our core purpose in order to make our lives more purposeful.

So you may wonder how do we energize these paths with a sense of purpose?

When we realize we have a certain quality of life and the talent to hopefully develop it even further, we can freely strive to fulfill the purpose for which we have these advantages and talents in the first place. We can also answer our calling to be involved in causes that appeal to us.

The challenge then is to remember to use our resources to elevate the world around us at least in proportion to the success we have attained. When we strive to support our business associates (or employees) fairly, deal honestly in business matters, and give appropriate charitable gifts to support our community and worthwhile causes, all while keeping our family as a top priority, then we are fulfilling a real purpose with our success.

We all have the opportunity to take the raw materials we deal with daily and improve on them. Part of that raw material can also be talents we have, opportunities that await us, and situations that need our input. We are part of the human destiny of making this world a better place for ourselves and for future generations. This sense of purpose can energize us for the long-term in a way personal benefit alone cannot always accomplish.

There is nothing wrong with working hard and honestly to attain considerable wealth, success, and/or fame. However, there should be a rightful purpose motivating us; one which reaches beyond our personal benefit or adding zeros on to our balance sheet. We must use these gifts in a way that helps "fix the world" and improve the lives of others.

*Profit is not the legitimate purpose of
business. The legitimate purpose of business
is to provide a product or service that people
need and do it so well that it's profitable.*
—James Rouse

Whether fulfilling our real purpose means having a job that enables us to help others, volunteering our time and talents, doing something that makes the world a better place, or giving charity to help another human being, all contribute to that purpose.

When we are in charge of our money/success/fame (and they are not in charge of us), we can direct our lives and better fulfill our purpose, as we should aspire to do. We must always remember that material goals are simply a means to an end; they are important enablers that provide needed ingredients in our life, but they are incomplete by themselves. Losing sight of this fact would mean exchanging the end for the means.

The most important attitudinal change in such a life is to realize that real "success" in life is measured by how well we are fulfilling our unique purpose. Knowing we are fulfilling our purpose will help us succeed in our job and our family life. It can also spare us from many of the common pitfalls which make striving for success so risky.

Living a life of purpose does not guarantee success in anything, but it can change our attitude toward striving for, or enjoying, success.

Make your work to be in keeping with your purpose.
—Leonardo da Vinci

Most people who have success in life, and who face few obstacles, realize nevertheless that there may be many potential pitfalls. Depending on their circumstances, these can include:

- balancing time priorities
- maintaining a happy and fulfilling home life
- pursuing personal and social interests
- raising well-adjusted children with solid values
- dealing with challenges at work, including dealing with employees/superiors or covering payroll

The "blessing" of not having any major challenges in life can also lead a person to a sense of aimlessness if not handled properly. We see it too often with, for example, children who are spoon-fed anything they want. When life gets boring and the challenge is not there, the monotony can drive us to make some poor decisions, and then we can journey into unhealthy places.

Similarly, purposeless materialism can lead people to be totally distracted from their purpose, leading some down a path of selfishness, addictions, or hedonism.

Without a proper anchor to guide us, it is too easy to fall victim to transforming success into a curse. The DNA of purpose in many people requires direction and a sense of fulfillment. Most of us need to find some meaning at every stage of life, even in small areas, so that our inner sense of purpose stays connected.

Success and wealth are blessings that can come or go without any advance notice. When we enjoy them, we can feel on top of the world, but in a life of purpose we have to remember that everything happens for a purpose. There is a reason why we are blessed this way, when we all know that there are other people, smarter and more qualified than us, who were not.

The secret of success is constancy of purpose.
—Benjamin Disraeli P

Now let's deal with the tough reality that many of us do live with on a daily basis.

What happens to our sense of purpose when we encounter, or live with, obstacles or challenges which in some small or large way cause us real problems in our life?

How are the billions of people who are not happy with aspects of their life scripts supposed to fulfill their purpose?

What about those who face serious health issues themselves or in their families, whether they are medical, psychiatric, or emotional?

Doesn't it make sense that the economic problems that challenge so many people around the globe, especially in third-world countries, undermine their ability to lead full and purposeful lives?

Don't relationship problems and/or emotional scars create obstacles to fulfilling a purpose?

Wouldn't personality shortcomings and/or addictions compromise our ability to fulfill our purpose in life?

*In a life of purpose, the answer is a resounding **NO!***

To the contrary, the full gamut of our challenges, tests and obstacles guide us to better connect to our individual purpose, because they help us define and fulfill our unique purpose. We can find great meaning in our lives through our struggle to meet daily challenges, and in so doing, achieve our fullest potential.

Most often we choose to fulfill a purpose in life in our way, within our limitations and, for the most part, within our comfort zone. We try to avoid or minimize the challenges we face in life.

However, when we deal directly with life's varied tests and obstacles we fulfill a purpose that pushes or forces us to better our world in ways we would normally not choose to do.

When our son Boruch was born with CF, I couldn't imagine that there could be any positive spin on his condition. It took years of "stretching my bungee cord" to realize that **we don't always define our purpose but rather life often defines our purpose for us.** When I grew to incorporate this new 'unwanted' purpose into my life, I could then see his sickness and all that came with it as an integral part of our purpose.

The manner in which we react to our challenges can help define the kind of person we are and the kind of life we lead. We can view an obstacle as a necessary evil, or find the strength to accept that it is part and parcel of the purpose of our life and then work to make the situation better (as described in greater length in chapter 7).

In addition, when we view the imperfections in our lives as meaningful pieces of our life puzzle, we then have an edge in dealing with life's ups and downs. In a sense we are connecting to reality on a deeper level. We are going beyond knee-jerk reactions. We aspire to operate in "flow mode" as opposed to "victim mode."

An aborigine walks into a surgical theater and witnesses a group of white-clad men and women leaning over a body, one brandishing a knife; a child is angry at his parents for allowing the dentist to pull his tooth; a friend seems to have betrayed your trust by visiting your opponent. None of these situations can be understood by viewing them superficially.

Events in our lives cannot be judged by their appearance. Life is like an onion with many layers, and we just need to keep peeling. The challenges of our lives force us to dig deeper.

In place of feelings of entitlement, we should expect obstacles to come our way and strive to surmount them. As an alternative to simply taking a positive attitude toward life's shortcomings, we should find meaning in them.

Jack and Stephanie were married after a two-year engagement. They both had great jobs and looked forward to promising careers, but after the birth of their first child, Stephanie fell into a long-term postpartum depression. John knew he was in for a major change in his life. He could either face this challenge with resentment or accept that his current purpose in life was to lovingly help his wife to recover. He chose the latter.

A life of purpose inspires us to see all imperfections as opportunities for us to go beyond our limits and, one hopes, create meaningful personal growth while making the world a better place. This is a powerful combination which can potentially elevate the challenges we face in all the other seven paths.

This is the fifth path - *treating all of the tests, obstacles and challenges of our life as important ingredients in fulfilling our life purpose.*

In conclusion, based on the explanations above, the positives and the negatives in our lives have one simple thing in common: they are all part of our life, and we must take ownership of all of them. Each has the potential, in their own unique way, to help us fulfill our purpose or to distract us from it. Ultimately there is no dichotomy, just choices of how we view the contrasts and extremes in life.

In other words, we do have the choice to see the circumstances of our life as having a purpose or not. We simply need to fine-tune our antennas to connect to our purpose, to be better prepared to make these choices.

PURPOSE PATHS

MAKE THE WORLD A BETTER PLACE

MAKE THE CIRCUMSTANCES OF OUR LIFE BETTER, IN ALL THEIR DETAILS

PROCREATION

SURVIVAL

TREAT THE VARIED OBSTACLES, CONFLICTS, AND TESTS IN LIFE AS BEING PART OF OUR UNIQUE PURPOSE

Chapter Three
The Path of Inner Change

For some people the most important area of accomplishing an individual purpose is in improving something in the world at large. Others work towards improving the circumstances of life around them, including their family, job and community. Still others focus on the many obstacles they face in life.

However all of us have the purpose to be engaged in bettering ourselves as people.

We all need to pay attention to, and improve, what is going on inside of us. **This is the sixth path,** *which focuses on developing our attitudes and personality.* After all, we are part of the world that needs fixing. In fact often it is much harder to fix ourselves than to fix some situation in the world around us.

For some people fixing themselves is a necessary step before they aspire to change the world. It may even be a required step before they feel a purpose in survival and procreation.

Jed had been abused by an uncle from the age of six. It left deep scars that undermined his self-esteem and deadened his desire to live. It took him years, but finally he gathered the energy and confidence to publicly confront his uncle at a family gathering. Only then did he begin to realize the full effect his scars had on him, and he began to discover how life could be a positive and purposeful experience.

The path of inner change helps us understand how a life of purpose potentially affects many aspects of our outlook on life. What attitudinal changes can take place when we start to live a life of purpose? How will we process or react to events of our life differently when we strive to see things from a purpose perspective?

The path of inner change is an important step toward leading a Purpose-Based Life (PBLife), and it can contribute greatly to an individual's intellectual, emotional, physical, and spiritual health. In a 2018 MedicalNewsToday.com article Maria Cohut writes that "having—or lacking—a life purpose, science has shown, can affect our mental and physical health in numerous and tangible ways…. The more we live with purpose, the more our bodies' stress-related aging processes are slowed down. It comes as no surprise, then, that there is a positive correlation between having a life purpose and enjoying longevity.[7] A type of traditional psychotherapy called logotherapy focuses on helping people become more aware of what makes their lives meaningful, so that they can overcome the obstacles affecting their quality of life more easily." (8)

---

[7]   The relationship of purpose and longevity is backed up by another study uploaded on May 24, 2019 at https://www.newsweek.com/people-sense-purpose-live-longer-study-suggests-1433771.

A sense of purpose can, with attention and patience, become second nature for us—a natural part of how we live and think. It does not need to drive our lives to the point that we become consumed by it or constantly have to second guess ourselves. It should lead to a balanced life whereby we can incorporate purpose in whatever daily activities we choose.

The choice is ours as to how much time and effort we want to put into it, although the potential is limitless.

> Kathy was very curious about purpose and had done lots of reading, but repeatedly saw the term 'driven' connected to purpose. She was not a driven person and thought perhaps that she could not really fulfill her purpose properly. Not until she heard about the eight paths did she realize that she could relate to purpose on her terms and did not have to conform to a relationship with purpose that for her would have been unnatural.

Following is a look at only four sample areas of a purpose-based life— personality (PBPersonality), relationships (PBRelationships), ethics (PBEthics) and happiness (PBHappiness). They provide a taste of how a purpose based life can affect our views in other areas of life as well.

PURPOSE-BASED PERSONALITY

We are often taught to see our behavior simply as the product of our environment and genetics (nature and nurture). Too often this becomes an excuse for actions that are counterproductive to a purposeful lifestyle.

Ted had been going to a therapist for years and was very comfortable with her approach to his life. He was then given an opportunity at work that excited and scared him at the same time. When discussing it with his therapist, she was lukewarm about it, concerned that his long-established issues and inner obstacles would potentially undermine his ability to rise to the challenge. Ted knew he would have to change some of his behaviors, but felt in his gut that he had what it took to accept the promotion. He also realized that his therapist had created a glass ceiling for his life and career. This discovery changed and motivated him to prove that he was not the prisoner of his past and could rise above his obstacles. He never looked back and went on to find hidden talents that came only as a result of going out of his comfort zone.

Ideally, fulfilling our purpose should come with an inner struggle. The battleground for this struggle takes place in the arenas of our thought, speech, and action (9). This struggle has a positive effect on our personality, because it pushes us to develop in ways we would have otherwise avoided. As a result, honest self-awareness and taking responsibility in these three arenas are crucial to being able to truly take charge of our life and fulfill our purpose.

Following are some very basic examples of how a life of purpose can give us a new perspective on challenges in our personality.

Anger can be better managed by searching to find a purpose for the events that enrage us. Negativity and depression can be addressed by realizing that events in our life are there to elevate us, not take us down.

Often our frustrations are in direct proportion to our expectations, and a more realistic understanding of how we have a purpose in facing the shortcomings and obstacles of life can relieve that effect.

Cultivating this ability to accept difficult situations that we find ourselves in also helps to reduce stress. Showing compassion to others even when we face hardships helps us to go beyond our personal needs to rise to a greater purpose.

The purpose of the personality challenges we face is to push us to exercise real free choice and stretch ourselves in some way, as discussed in greater depth in chapter 7. A purpose-based personality realizes that often the most difficult challenges we face are the ones that offer the greatest potential for personal change and for fulfilling our long-term purpose.

All these challenges push us to focus on the sometimes raw personality we have and then rise to develop our true human potential. Living a life of purpose can provide the tools to neutralize the poison of harmful emotions that can paralyze us.

For some of us this process could take years or even a lifetime. When we persevere and go beyond our basic instincts and nature, we are exercising free choice in its purest form and making the small world of "I" a better place to be in.

PURPOSE-BASED RELATIONSHIPS

A purpose-based relationship has to develop and mature over a period of time and cannot artificially add a layer of purpose in an unnatural manner. Relationships need to be real and sincere, especially when dealing with our immediate family, and any ulterior motive connected to a purpose can undermine the trust needed in a meaningful relationship.[8] Hence I wouldn't suggest a person read this book and go home to impose its thoughts on his or her family members and friends. We don't need to fix anybody but ourselves in a relationship. As my wife often reminds me, sometimes she just wants her issues to be heard, not to be fixed. Simply enjoying the company of our immediate family is a top priority in fulfilling our individual purpose.

It is important to note that not everything in life has to be permeated with the pursuit of purpose. Love, sincerity, and compassion are positive powers which stand on their own. They all serve an important purpose when they naturally motivate us to action in any or all of the eight paths of purpose. They automatically make the world a better place for the recipients of the love and the compassion.

There are many areas in which the pursuit of purpose can help a person be aware of how to improve human relations, both in business, in marriage, and in personal life. Most important of these is the area of communication.

When I want to make a point, is my purpose to say what's on my mind or to get my point across in a receptive and effective manner? Should I try to prove to my spouse that I am right, or find a mutually agreed-upon solution? Do I want to tell my children how upset I am, or do I want them to be better people?

Some of these situations can be very emotional, and it requires tremendous self-control to keep our focus on the purpose of our conversation. In the case of business, focusing on the purpose of a conversation can be a crucial measure of success. In personal life, it can define us as being either compassionate and empathetic or arrogant and out of touch.

---

8   For more on this topic see chapter 5, point #6.

Being aware of our personality includes "owning our position" in any relationship and being prepared to take total responsibility for the effect we have on people. It means accepting that the people in our life are who they are for a very important reason, and each can teach us something important about our purpose. It means realizing that even hurtful situations have a purpose. Holding resentment or anger only hurts us. Forgiveness almost always has a worthwhile purpose.

Striving to develop a PBRelationship also opens us up to seeing a purpose in exploring friendships with people we may meet on a flight or in the local park and to being respectful of that one out of seven billion human beings whom we encounter driving the city bus, especially since our lives may depend on that person.

It also means respecting the power of time, either as a healer or as part of the complex process needed to get from A to B or Z in any relationship. When we rush aspects of any relationship and try to force results, we are not allowing the purpose of the relationship to run its full course.

Most important of all, living a life of purpose empowers us that when we are brought into contact with another person, we can use the opportunity to somehow better the situation we both find ourselves in.

PURPOSE-BASED ETHICS

A general ethos in a purpose-based life is to do our best to fulfill our unique purpose. A person could easily think, "I am fulfilling purpose #3 and #4 by raising a family and working very hard to provide for them and this is the limit of what I can do" or "If I volunteer once in a while at the local nursing home I'm a good person and doing my part" or "I have too many problems to start thinking about other people."

In some situations all those statements may be true; however, the large majority of us, especially in democratic countries, have the freedom and opportunity to take our purpose far beyond a minimalist commitment. We all have the inner wiring and the personal tools to have a positive influence on our environment. If we fall short of doing what we can do to make the world a better place, then in reality we are not truly fulfilling our unique purpose.

In addition, in a PBLife, ethics in general are not just a matter of right and wrong; they provide direction for judging how to fulfill our purpose in any particular situation.

When life places us in a situation and we realize that an ethical decision must be made, purpose-based ethics (PBEthics) sees that this event is taking place in some sense for us to fulfill a purpose.

> Edith was doing her weekly shopping trip and found all the items she wanted. When checking her out, the cashier was distracted and skipped an expensive item. Edith was at first not sure whether to speak up but then realized that her personal integrity was more important than a dress and pointed out the mistake. After returning home she was quite proud of her instincts.

A PBLife is ethics-oriented and sees events in life as an opportunity to improve the world, not make it worse. Each situation in which we face a moral conflict or dilemma is often the juxtaposition and result of a complex series of many events. We, not our neighbor or cousin, are the ones found in the middle, which gives us an opportunity to enhance the fulfillment of our purpose.

Lying or cheating are attempts to deceive ourselves into thinking we can change or hide from the realities of the life that we are meant to lead at any given moment. The attempt to then try to benefit from this deception is the opposite of fulfilling our purpose. Honesty and interpersonal trust are important keys to living with purpose. Dealing in an ethical manner with the sometimes complex changes in life that we encounter from moment to moment is fundamental.

Similarly, jealousy removes us from our true reality and is an obstacle to developing PBEthics. Comparing our tools in life with those of anyone else is a sign that we are out of touch with our purpose for having what we have at this moment. When we feel that we don't have exactly what we are supposed to have because somebody else has more, we are denying the purpose of what we do have.

Once we accept our life in all its details and take full ownership of it, there is nothing wrong with striving for more. But the purpose of acquiring more is not to catch up with somebody else, but rather to provide a means to the end of better fulfilling our unique purpose in life.

Our weaknesses can become strengths. People with a tendency toward jealousy, constantly looking to see what material possessions others have, can harness that tendency to seek out the good personality qualities others may possess, and be inspired to better their own life as a result.

In business a lack of ethics can not only be illegal, but also sap the motivation and sense of purpose from otherwise dedicated employees. There is no shortage of studies about the trickle effect that a lack of ethics of the top brass can have on the whole company.

Those who are involved in government or the legal/justice system have a special merit and responsibility to ensure that society functions with a strong ethical foundation.[9]

Without ethics, it is possible for people to rationalize that they can do whatever it takes to fulfill their own purpose at the expense of another person's purpose or society at large.

PBEthics are an important scenario for the exercise of free choice, because in many situations we are not programmed to be ethical, but we go beyond our nature to do what we know and believe to be right, even if it could involve personal loss.

Purpose-Based Happiness

Without my knowing it, as a child I was in the process of developing a life plan. We all are. Based on what we absorb from our home and environment, we create specific ways for dealing with life. As with any child, I was combining what I learned from my parents, my teachers, my friends and my environment to figure out how to live the best life I could. As the years went by and my childhood became a distant memory, the life plan I formulated was put to the test by the many complexities of life.

At that time "life, liberty, and the pursuit of happiness" seemed to be the bywords society lived with. Life was wonderful. Liberty was simple enough: I enjoyed doing whatever I wanted to do in our democracy. Then there was happiness. I was happy, so that seemed pretty simple too. Everybody wants to be happy, so why not pursue it?

But as time went on, I realized it wasn't so simple. I saw that many people were not happy, even though they went to great lengths to pursue

---

9   This principle is one of the Seven Universal Laws for the nations of the world to work toward the establishment of a just society. Visit asknoah.org for more information.

happiness. I found myself in situations where feelings were hurt, and sometimes I was the cause. As much as I tried to be happy, it wasn't always working. The problem seems to be that as we grow older, we take on so much baggage that we disconnect from our inherent happy nature.

I remember that as a child I never had to pursue happiness; it happened naturally. Happiness was not a goal in life. I was happy as a result of the relationships I had and the environment my parents worked hard to create.

Over the years I learned, as do most people, that happiness cannot be attained through acquiring "things." Dependency on outside stimuli, and the pursuit of pleasure or fun, gives us only a fleeting sense of happiness. When we are dependent on material possessions and fun to achieve happiness, we are constantly searching for something (or someone) that will keep us happy or make us even happier. This quest can lead to some very dangerous and damaging pursuits. The problem we face is that often the more we pursue happiness, the more elusive it becomes (10).

I decided that if I wanted to be happy in a real way, I would have to develop it from the inside out. I had to differentiate between fun, which I enjoyed, and happiness, which takes real work. More importantly, I had to stop pursuing happiness and adopt a way of life that would produce inner happiness as a by-product.

What kind of happiness fits that description?

Inner happiness is a natural by-product of a life lived with purpose. This comes from a sense of fulfillment which we potentially feel whenever our life reality and/or attitude are aligned in some way with our life purpose.

I do not claim that this is the only way to reach true happiness, but I do believe that there is no greater inner contentment than having the sense that you are fulfilling your unique purpose in life. In fact, pursuing purpose results in a lasting happiness even more than "the pursuit of happiness" does.

When we are at peace with fulfilling our purpose, the happiness radiates out from deep within. We know this fact to be true, because even when the circumstances of our life are not consistent with the usual causes for happiness, we can still feel an inner happiness by doing something that we feel is consistent with our life purpose.

This type of happiness can be accomplished only when it is specifically a by-product. If happiness is even a secondary goal in a life of purpose, it can taint the purpose we are fulfilling and most likely will not produce true inner happiness. For instance, when we fulfill a purpose, there may be circumstances that can often cause the opposite of happiness. If happiness is even a secondary goal, our willpower could easily be weakened, potentially creating obstacles to fulfilling the purpose.

Jack and Dorothy were both told by their doctors in no uncertain terms that they had to lose weight. They decided to join Weight Watchers together and took it very seriously. With time they both succeeded in reaching their first goal, but Jack started to lose interest, stating that it was no longer fun. Dorothy tried to explain to him that they were not doing this for fun, and that she felt a deep sense of accomplishment from it. She tried to convince Jack that their longevity depended on it, but Jack didn't buy it, and he dropped out. It seems that Jack related to weight loss as a specific goal to create happiness, while Dorothy saw it as a process with a bigger purpose.

True inner happiness is simply the result of an independent journey that precedes it. Fulfilling our purpose should not be a means to an end of being happy.

> *Happiness is a by-product of function, purpose, and conflict; those who seek happiness for itself seek victory without war.*
> —William S. Burroughs

As important as happiness is, it is not a purpose path of its own. Inner happiness can be the result of each of the eight paths.

When we volunteer to help others, donate to a good cause, or do an act of kindness, the good feeling we have as a by-product is not just hormonal. When people are depressed, sometimes they are advised to go out and visit a hospital. It's not just a feel-good therapy or "it could be worse" approach. We are actually connecting to our core in a deep way that gives us an inner sense of purpose and happiness.

I have met many people whose economic status would define them as poor, but they are very happy individuals. Similarly there are many wealthy people who have not figured out a path to happiness.

Attaining a positive, purposeful attitude in life is not good just for us personally, but can also have a very positive effect on our family, our job, and our relationships. Instead of being dependent on them for our happiness, which can place an extra weight on any relationship, we bring happiness to them.

Melissa was a star teacher in middle school and enjoyed everything about her job, but as a healthy and curious fifty-five-year-old, she also had dreamed of retirement for years. She looked forward to doing all the things she couldn't do as a teacher and had a wish list that would take decades to finish. As retirement came closer, though, she started to have second thoughts. She slowly realized that there was something very deep inside of her that she was getting from teaching that she would be giving up by following only her wish list. She had a sense of purpose and a feeling of accomplishment that together created an inner happiness she did not want to lose. She realized about herself that the drive for life she felt every day was largely the result of her firm belief that she was changing lives and making a better future for the world at large. It was a very difficult decision, but she withdrew her retirement papers. Instead of a retirement party, she held a re-hirement party for her colleagues and students.

In a life of purpose, inner happiness comes not despite the challenges of life, but in response to them.

Realizing that the imperfections of our life are there for a purpose makes them a partner in the challenges of life, not an enemy.

A purposeful outlook also puts to rest the question of "what if" that often robs us of inner balance and happiness. As the saying goes, "There is no greater happiness than freeing oneself of doubts."

Acceptance of ourselves and our circumstances in life affords the ability to be happy with what we have. We focus on the good in our lives—on what we have instead of what we don't have. We accept our imperfections and know we will never be perfect. We accept that what we have at the end of the day is what we need to fulfill our purpose today.(11)

Tomorrow we can go out and conquer the world anew, but for this moment, we are whole.

A lawyer, a doctor, and a teacher were in a Siberian prison. To everyone's bafflement the teacher was always happy. The lawyer and doctor approached him to ask how he could possibly be happy in that dismal place. He asked them why they were unhappy. The lawyer answered that he was once very successful, but after giving bad advice to a high-ranking member of the Communist Party, he was sentenced to ten years. The doctor said that he was thrown into prison for misdiagnosing a member of the politburo. The teacher explained that he was sentenced for teaching, but he was happy fulfilling his life's purpose in Moscow and was still doing the same—except under a different set of circumstances.

When my wife and I were in the hospital with our son for weeks, we came to realize that we had no control over anything in our lives—except for our attitude. Nobody and nothing could force us to have a negative and pessimistic view of our situation. As much as natural instincts would dictate otherwise, we knew we had the free choice to maintain a positive attitude and remain happy and positive in our heavily burdened lives. When we exercised our free choice to overcome a natural negativity, we felt a palpable sense of inner accomplishment.

Choice gives us the power to be happy on a daily basis (see chapter 7), even in the most trying of circumstances (see chapter 8) despite what our nature may dictate and what others might think or say ("...he is in denial."). In fact the happiness we develop from a life of purpose helps us make better choices by striving to go beyond our nature. As the saying goes, "Happiness breaks through boundaries." This inner peace energizes us and provides us with an anchor through the rough as well as the calm waters of life.

Inner happiness is not only a benefit of a life of purpose; it is part of the DNA of purpose. A life of purpose without inner happiness is missing an important ingredient and needs to be reexamined.

How do we change our knee-jerk reactions? How do we apply these ideas to attain happiness? When we activate our willpower and choose our thoughts, speech, and actions on an ongoing basis, we can face challenges and changes with new energy and passion.

PURPOSE PATHS

MAKE THE WORLD A BETTER PLACE

MAKE THE CIRCUMSTANCES OF OUR LIFE BETTER, IN ALL THEIR DETAILS

PROCREATION

SURVIVAL

TREAT THE VARIED OBSTACLES, CONFLICTS AND TESTS IN LIFE AS BEING PART OF OUR UNIQUE PURPOSE

IMPROVE OUR INNER SELVES TO BE BETTER PEOPLE, WITH PURPOSE-BASED ATTITUDES

CHAPTER 4

Was It Meant to Happen?

This chapter is divided in two sections. This first section explores a purpose-based view of how to respond to events which happen around us: past, present or future. For some it is simply another path to fulfill our purpose to make the world a better place. For others this is a path which can also be part of a spiritual journey.

O ur lives are largely dominated by three major influences – our selves, our life circumstances, and our life experiences.

The seventh path of purpose can raise the bar significantly in a life of purpose. It is the path of *seeing events and experiences in our lives as an opportunity to create positive change*.

This path gives us the opportunity to truly make purpose a part of our daily lives. As will be further explained in greater depth in chapter 9, there are many situations throughout every day wherein we have the potential to affect our lives and the lives of those around us as well.

We all have the potential, and in some cases the obligation, to be a force for making our surroundings better as events around us constantly change. It is simply up to us to choose to step up to the plate. The opportunities are limitless.

This path differs from the second path in that this path focuses on the changing events and experiences of our daily life, while the second path focuses on improving the general circumstances of our life and our immediate surroundings. This is a very different application of 'making the world a better place'. It challenges us to seek opportunities through our interactions with people and things, to try to improve or make better a situation we see could benefit from our positive input.

However, there is also a more spiritual dimension to this path, which does overlap with the second path, and helps us to see that there may actually be a purpose *why* we encounter both the events and the circumstances of the life that we lead.

Let's explore this more.

When was the last time you found yourself saying, "It was meant to happen?" Was it in amazement, with your jaw dropped, as events were unfolding before your eyes? Or was it about something that happened days, months, or even years before? Was it the ultimate aha moment— when you realized that a seemingly insignificant event led to the resolution of a longstanding problem or a great opportunity? Perhaps you stood scratching your head about a coincidence that could hardly have happened by chance. Or was the event so unusual that the statement "it was meant to happen" was the only way to explain it?

At such moments we feel we are touching a different dimension of reality, one we rarely experience. We feel that some things actually do happen for a purpose, and it can give us a warm, secure feeling inside that on some level there is a positive force causing these events. It's one of the mysteries of life that we cherish when we are privy to it.

Is it possible that other events are also meant to happen, even if we don't experience that special feeling at the time? Are only the events that give us that special feeling the ones that are meant to happen? Do we have to see a sign or experience a coincidence to acknowledge that something in our life was meant to happen?

Maybe indeed other events in our lives were also meant to be, even though there was nothing particularly noticeable about them at the time. Perhaps they were too insignificant, distasteful, or painful for us to imagine that maybe they also were meant to happen.

Sometimes we feel a purpose when we see a situation we know we have the ability to improve upon. Sometimes events jump out at us as having a purpose for us to engage. They could be a chance encounter, coincidence, serendipity, or déjà vu. Perhaps our simple intuition or sixth sense tells us that there is a purpose behind a particular experience. It could be a discussion we have with our seatmate at the deli or another patient waiting in the doctor's office.

> *I truly believe that everything that we do and everyone that we meet is put in our path for a purpose. There are no accidents; we're all teachers—if we're willing to pay attention to the lessons we learn, trust our positive instincts, and are not afraid to take risks.*
> —MARLA GIBBS

Were we meant to be born to our particular set of parents and inherit our unique genetic makeup—the face we wear, the talents we have, the weight problems we struggle with, or the shortcomings of our personality? What about some of the events of our childhood—the sibling who had a powerful influence on our lives, the neighborhood we grew up in, or a third-grade teacher who inspired us?

Did an argumentative brother give us the skills needed to deal with our own child? Did a terrible experience lead us to discover an undeveloped talent? Was a childhood trauma the catalyst for choosing our future career?

Does the fact that we didn't take notice at the time mean it was *not* meant to happen?

Perhaps the emotional scars from childhood were not mistakes or random events. As painful as they may have been, they made us who we are today, hopefully giving us tools to empathize with others.

Taking ownership of the defects in one's personality and dealing with them is part of life's journey. It helps define life as well as the individual's purpose. It gives us the tools to make our unique imprint on this world and "fix" our small world as only we can.

All these are pieces of the puzzle that made me who I am and you who you are; so many of these we had absolutely no control over. To a lesser or greater degree, they all produced the person that we have become.

Is the person I am today the result of many random influences, or is there a deeper reason why I am who I am? Could it be that the many details of our lives, even the negative ones, were meant to happen?

And if it was meant to happen, doesn't that mean that it happened for some purpose? Why or how would it be meant to happen if there was no purpose behind it happening?

Writers—and I believe generally all persons—
must think that whatever happens to them
is a resource. All things have been given
to us for a purpose, and an artist must feel
this more intensely. All that happens to us,
including our humiliations, our misfortunes,
our embarrassments, all is given to us as raw
material, as clay, so that we may shape our art.
—JORGE LUIS BORGES, *TWENTY-FOUR CONVERSATIONS WITH*
BORGES: INTERVIEWS BY ROBERTO ALIFANO 1981-1983

This is how purpose works behind the scenes, making changes in our lives, for a purpose.

The objects and obstacles of the world we deeply desire to fix are determined not just by chance: there is purpose behind the encounter itself. We could even say that the encounter was meant to happen.

Let's try to understand this by exploring a different aspect of the dimension of purpose.

An early eighteenth-century rabbi once taught that everything in the world has a purpose. Every change that takes place has meaning. Even a leaf that falls from a tree in the forest and the path it takes to its point of landing also has a purpose.[10]

I was twenty years old when I first read this statement. I was fascinated that he could make such a radical claim. It seemed outlandish. If true, it infused an intense sense of purpose into every aspect of our world. If

---

10   From the teachings of Rabbi Israel Baal Shem (1698 – 1760), known as the Baal Shem Tov. After being orphaned at the age of five, he was raised by mystics in the forests of the Carpathian Mountains, where he did much meditation and eventually started the Chassidic Movement in Judaism. His wisdom and wonders fill the pages of many volumes and have inspired millions. He explained that the leaf falling on a worm accomplished an important purpose in shielding the worm from hungry birds. Not an important purpose for you and me, but for that worm it meant the world.

a falling leaf has a purpose, then other events in nature, and the world we live in, also have a purpose. It was one of the teachings that motivated me to want to learn more.

> *The leaf that captures a stream of sunlight,*
> *and then transfers its energy to the tree,*
> *serves one purpose in the spring and*
> *summer and another completely different*
> *one through the fall and winter.*
> —GUY FINLEY

I soon discovered that this attitude can energize us to see all the details of life from a new perspective. In the world of purpose "no man is an island" means that we are an organic and integral part of the environment we are living in, not just tourists who are passing through a particular situation.

We are meant to interact with our environment and our environment with us, bringing improvement to both. In fact, nature allows that most imperfections can be improved upon, most wounds can heal, most breaks can be fixed, and darkness can be dispelled by even a little light. Almost everything has the potential to change, and maybe even be fixed, given enough time and/or effort. We can be active players in many ways during our daily activities.

Rebbetzin Chaya M. Schneerson[11] would go with a driver to a park in Long Island. One day they found their regular route closed off because of road work and they were forced to take an alternate route. As they drove along they passed a woman on the side of the

---

11   the daughter of Rabbi Y. Y. Schneerson (1880-1950) and wife of Rabbi M. M. Schneerson (1902-1994), the sixth and seventh leaders of Chabad. Rebbetzin is a title for the wife of a rabbi.

road crying and protesting. The rebbetzin turned to the driver and said, "I heard a woman crying. Can you go back and see what that was about?" They turned around and saw workers carrying furniture from a house and loading it onto the truck of the county marshal. The marshal explained that the woman had not paid her rent for many months and was being evicted. The rebbetzin then inquired how much the woman owed and if the marshal could accept a personal check. The marshal said that he had no problem as long as he confirmed with the bank that the check was covered. She wrote out a check for the full amount and then urged the driver to quickly drive away. Amazed at what he had seen, the driver asked what had prompted her to give such a large sum to a total stranger. "Once when I was a young girl, my father took me for a walk in the park. He sat me down on a bench and told me, 'Every time something causes us to deviate from our normal routine, there is a reason for it.' Today when I saw the detour sign I remembered my father's words and immediately thought, 'Suddenly the street's closed off, and we're sent to a different street. What is the purpose of this? How is this connected to me?' Then I heard the sound of a woman crying and screaming. I realized that we had been sent along this route for a purpose" (12)

When we choose to see events of our life and the world around us as having purpose, we can then come to the realization that some of the ongoing changing circumstances in our lives and in the world we live in are also subtly providing the tools we need to fulfill our individual purpose.

This purpose path, whether we see it through spiritual glasses or not, can inspire all of us to fulfill our role in life and be an active participant in making our immediate world a better place. If we would try to be guided by this path even to a small degree, many new vistas would open up and the effect on our life would be significant.

PURPOSE - BASED FAITH

The second section of this chapter addresses readers who are comfortable with a faith-based approach to purpose. A faith-based approach connotes a belief in a Higher Power and/or a particular religious path.

A life of purpose can reach additional new heights for those who believe a Higher Power is active in their lives. In fact for millennia religions of the world have inspired people to make purpose a part of their lives.

When we can accept that a perfect God deliberately created a very imperfect world and that each of us has an important and unique purpose in perfecting it, we are better equipped to deal with the myriad imperfections of life. It is God who provides us with the tools we need to fulfill our purpose on all levels.

In fact, God created mankind with all the following totally unique attributes so that we can better achieve our purpose:

1. The paradox of purpose whereby we don't inherently know our purpose in life
2. The DNA of purpose in our core being which whispers to us to want to make our lives, and the world at large, better for us and future generations

3. The intelligence, free choice and willpower to activate and connect to our purpose with intent

4. The ability to achieve a deep inner happiness as a result of fulfilling our purpose in life, sometimes while overcoming great challenges

This combination of unique attributes creates a Godly and balanced mosaic which potentially challenges us all to be the best person we can be.

In addition, the belief in a soul that God has put in each of us for a unique purpose adds tremendous perspective for understanding why purpose is the hidden dimension that has so much influence on our lives. Each soul serves as a channel through which God grants a unique life force for every individual in the world. Each soul comes to this world for a unique purpose and makes its unique contribution to the world, which accounts for why no two people are the same.

Hence, each soul encounters the imperfections of the world it needs to improve upon, including all the positive and negative tools it must have to accomplish its purpose in coming into its particular body, family, and community. When we realize that our lives and the world are "perfectly imperfect," and the events of our life are "meant to happen", we can take ownership of the imperfections we have and realize that they are all custom made for us to better fulfill our purpose.

> *Whoever has faith in individual Divine*
> *Providence knows that "man's steps are established*
> *by God," that this particular soul must purify and*
> *improve something specific in a particular place.*
> *For centuries, or even since the world's creation,*
> *that which needs purification or improvement*
> *waits for this soul to come and purify or improve*
> *it. The soul too, has been waiting—ever since*
> *it came into being—for its time to descend, so*
> *that it can discharge the tasks of purification*
> *and improvement assigned to it. (13)*
> —Rabbi M.M. Schneerson

When our son died, it was our belief in a soul that personally gave me the most strength and comfort. Part of this belief is that his soul came to this world for a purpose; he accomplished that purpose in his short thirteen years of life and then continued his soul journey.

For those who ask why he had to go through such suffering and live such a short life, I truly believe that there is a purpose which God knows, one which the soul discovers after death.

Living with purpose can also add a new dimension to a relationship with the Creator. God is not some removed Being who watches or runs the world from a distance, but rather a unifying force that can be felt on a very personal level.

This God is intimately involved in every detail of our lives, both the positive and seemingly negative, and is the One who provides all the raw material we need to accomplish our purpose. Thus, Divine Providence can be an active dimension in a life of purpose.

Ultimately it is God alone who truly knows the purpose of our lives and the events that happen around us. In a relationship with God, it is this belief that can help us develop trust that everything an infinite God does is ultimately for a good purpose, even when we can't comprehend it. These beliefs also infuse new meaning into all of the paths of purpose.

Religions of the world provide a great variety of means, whether through inspiration and/or repentance, by which billions of people better connect to God and to their universal purpose in life in a very meaningful way, and we can hope they enrich and intensify a sense of purpose with great depth. Each religion does this in a unique way.

The Five Books of Moses—the source of so many Judeo-Christian-Muslim values—teaches that the purpose of all humanity is for all peoples of the world together to better this world in God's image.

For this reason, and since religions and belief in a Higher Power have inspired so many to fulfill a purpose in life by making the world a better place, I count this—*connecting to a Higher Power to elevate ourselves and the world*—**as the eighth path of purpose**.

For many religions, all eight paths described in this book are really connected under one Higher Path—fulfilling the will of God and giving God pleasure, which can motivate us and serve as a driving force to fulfill all eight paths. For me this is the most powerful means by which all of humanity can "fix the world" by connecting it and ourselves to the Creator of the universe, as outlined in the Five Books of Moses.[12]

---

12   The Five Books of Moses (Torah) gives specific commandments (mitzvahs) to all humanity. These commandments provide the specific tools needed, from God's perspective, to elevate and change the world and ourselves in a positive way. The ancient Jewish commentators take it one step further. They explain that by being an active participant in this process of fixing the world, we become actual partners with the Creator of the universe (14). The Creator wants this world to become a better world—even a perfect world—but wants it to happen through the efforts of all of humanity. God

Whatever your religion may be, there is no greater sense of inner happiness than to believe that you are actually playing a key role in accomplishing the purpose God made for the world and for you, while giving God pleasure in the process.

"desired to have a dwelling place in this lower world," (15) and when God deems the world is ready, we will experience the Messianic Era. Our good deeds are not just for the sake of making the world a better place or for a personal reward. They will all culminate in the eventual victory of light over darkness, good over evil, and the fulfillment of an ultimate purpose. All these ideas are consistent with biblical teachings.

THE EIGHT PURPOSE PATHS

MAKE THE WORLD A BETTER PLACE

MAKE THE CIRCUMSTANCES OF OUR LIFE BETTER, IN ALL THEIR DETAILS

PROCREATION

SURVIVAL

TREAT THE VARIED OBSTACLES, CONFLICTS AND TESTS IN LIFE AS BEING PART OF OUR UNIQUE PURPOSE

IMPROVE OUR INNER SELVES TO BE BETTER PEOPLE, WITH PURPOSE-BASED ATTITUDES

SEE MANY OF THE EVENTS OF OUR DAILY LIVES AS OPPORTUNITIES TO BRING ABOUT POSITIVE CHANGE

CONNECT TO OUR HIGHER POWER AND/OR RELIGION TO ELEVATE OURSELVES AND THE WORLD AROUND US

CHAPTER FIVE
Eight Purpose Pointers

*A*s we try to round out our overview of how purpose thinks, it is time to address some common questions and relevant issues. Following is a collection of eight tips that will help to clarify how to live a life of purpose. It offers some interesting topics for conversation with your friends and family.

1. Understanding purpose takes patience

In a life of purpose we must live with a combination of ongoing curiosity, amazement, and frustration. The fact that we are surrounded by events happening for a purpose does not mean that we can interpret all events in our life in real time in an attempt to figure out their purpose on the spot.

We can look back in time to see the major events and turning points of our life, as well as the ongoing challenges we face, to see a unique pattern. We can explore an overall purpose for why we have a particular personality defect or talent and what we are meant to do with it.

We can identify a past event as having served an important long-term purpose and decide whether we have developed it to its fullest. We can even throw ourselves into a sudden opportunity or responsibility because we see how in tune it is with our ethics, goals, and core values, and we need to step up to the plate.

Sometimes events in our lives beckon us to follow a certain path, or make certain decisions, and it is clear to us that this is where we need to be. Our intuition, and friends, can usually guide us well in this area.

However, actually figuring out the purpose of most specific events or coincidences in our life at the time they are happening can be difficult and sometimes misleading.

My wife once met a handicapped woman who told her the following story. She had been waiting for a wheelchair-accessible city bus on a freezing night. The first bus passed right by her. The second bus stopped, but the driver refused to be bothered with operating the handicapped access lift. She was freezing and livid. Fortunately fifteen minutes later another bus came by, and the driver helped her on. When she got to the bus depot, she reported the second driver to the dispatcher. She was shocked to hear that soon after he had left her out in the cold, his bus had lost electricity and still had not returned to the station. Upon hearing this news, her whole attitude changed. She realized that if that driver had picked her up, she would have had no way of getting off the bus.

Another woman told me about her husband's untimely death from a staph infection after minor surgery. She was angry at God, the hospital, and herself. Two months later the results of the autopsy showed that he had early stages of pancreatic cancer, a virtual death sentence at that time, which brings with it great suffering. Despite her grief, her anger was replaced by relief.

A purpose was at work in both those experiences. The first was a one-time event; the second was a life-altering one. In one it took thirty minutes to be privy to the purpose. In the other it took two months. In each case once a purpose behind the event came to the surface, it totally changed the women's perceptions. Purpose was an integral part of the scenario from the beginning, but the women were not privy to it at the time. It may be thirty days, months, or years before we understand the reason something happened to us, and only then does it become clear to us that it was really meant to be.

Very often we will never know the reason, but that doesn't mean there was no purpose at all; quite possibly there is a reason for our not knowing the purpose.

There is a fable about a man who wished to know the language of the birds. He heard of a great sage who knew their language, but the sage refused to teach him. The man gave him no peace until the sage finally agreed. One fine day the man heard the birds chirping, and with his newly acquired knowledge, he understood them say, "This man has burglars in his house." He ran home, caught the burglars red-handed, and succeeded in chasing them away. Sometime later, he again heard the birds speaking about him. "This man has a fire in his house." He dashed home and to his relief was able to minimize the damage. The next conversation he overheard was the birds saying "See that man? He will die in two weeks." In shock he ran to the sage and begged him to save his life. The sage told him, "You were never meant to understand the language of the birds. Because you learned their language, you will not

> fully experience certain events that would help you fulfill your life's purpose. There is nothing I can do to help you."

Sometimes we just have to experience something to fulfill our purpose—no reasons needed, no understanding available. It is what it is, without any choice in the matter. At best, we may be able to learn a lesson from the experience.

As we learn more and more about the sciences, we see how interdependent all of existence is—how the smallest of actions can have a ripple effect that may take many years to come to the surface, like an hourglass with thousands of grains of sand having to fall into place over time. A pear tree will bear fruit only after five or six years of internal development; when a volcano erupts or an earthquake occurs, it can be the result of hundreds of years of pressure building up. A grudge, anger, or jealousy can sometimes take years to come to the surface and then explode with major repercussions. The same applies to the purpose behind events in our lives; many circumstances in our lives have their own hourglass, and it can take years for the purpose to come to the surface.

> Gloria was not the most social of people and was happiest in her own home. Her husband traveled frequently on business, and she accompanied him simply to accommodate him. On one occasion he asked her to come along with little notice, and she went reluctantly. Surprisingly she hit it off with her seatmate, Beth, a doctor who specialized in a rare pediatric disease, and they maintained contact for many years. Twenty-three years later, Gloria's daughter gave birth to a baby with

> that rare illness. Gloria then understood the purpose behind that fortuitous meeting. She could have dismissed it as a coincidence, but she could not shake the notion that their meeting was predestined.

Did you ever stop to think how many pieces of the puzzle had to fall into place for you to get your job, meet your spouse, or buy your house? Many events in your life are the result of a chain of events. There could even be multiple events that seem to be heading in one direction until they all come together for a seemingly unrelated purpose.

In a life with purpose, we stand at the center of a myriad of events that evolve to help us fulfill our unique purpose. The ripple effect of each action continues to create new circumstances. We just need the patience to be able to see purpose unfold as the ripple has time to expand.

2. Accept your reality, but do not be resigned to it

Even though there is purpose behind why we are who we are, it does not give us permission to be satisfied with the status quo. An "I'm OK; you're OK" attitude is not consistent with a life of purpose. We need to learn how to accept our reality with inner peace, but we should not be resigned to any reality that can be improved upon, especially in our close relationships.

We are meant to experience, learn from, and then ideally improve upon the world around and within. We should aspire to explore opportunities that come our way, fix the imperfections we encounter, and always try to make tomorrow better than today.

3. Know when to transition from a situation

A life of purpose helps us gain a clear vision so we can get to work on a strategy to take the next step in any situation. However, when life's many distractions cross our paths, we must be very discerning about what we put our energies into. Sometimes we can get involved in something, but after much effort or when an irreversible act happens or when we have tried every possible way to change something, we have to be able to say that "It is meant to be the way it is now, and let's move on." We have hit an unmovable wall and can't change the situation.

Such an event could be a health condition, a lost election or job, or the end of a relationship for which there is no more hope. It could be an adversary who can't be defeated or a business deal that has been fatally undermined. To put any more effort into trying to change an unchangeable circumstance would most likely be a waste of valuable energy.

Perhaps sometime in the future the situation will change, but for now we need to put our energies in other directions without anger, resentment, or revenge. Once we come to this conclusion, we need to shift gears toward fulfillment of a new purpose in relation to a newly defined situation. Our efforts then need to be more focused on personal adjustment to the new aspects of life.

Surely there was a purpose why we had to get involved in the first place and there was most likely a lesson to be learned. It was not a mistake or a waste of time. Who knows what the ripple effect of our past involvement will be in the future and how far it will go? It could be that the transition after this realization is part of the purpose for getting involved in the first place. Ideally sometime in the future we will be able to look back and see what purpose was served.

This transition could include emotional healing, finding a new direction in life, moving our home, or any of a number of new ventures. Most importantly it can mean making some serious adjustments in our family or personality to learn to flow with these new realities and not be victimized by them.

With all the above said, when the event that is "meant to be" involves our family, we are not always at liberty to transition away from the challenge, so we may need to get as much professional advice and help as possible.

4. Avoid doubt and hesitation

Don't spend your life wondering about the purpose of your life or reading into things. It is much more important to take meaningful action than to ponder for extended times. By the time you figure a situation out, everything may have changed and an opportunity could be lost.

We cannot understand our purpose for dealing with all the events in our life, so we have to act as best we can in response to events at the time we encounter them. Sure we may take risks, but when we use our best judgment, we can go into any situation with confidence. As long as we are guided by trying to make the world a better place, the worst that can happen is that we expend energy for a good cause.

For the millions who are by nature consumed with the question "Why me?" when put in difficult situations, I ask a simple question to ponder: you are not going to get an answer in this lifetime, so why hesitate when you can possibly have some small positive effect on improving the circumstances?

5. The role of self-actualization

As discussed in chapter 1, there is a significant difference between self-actualization and fulfilling your purpose in life.

Purpose is often about what is greater than "self." When a situation calls for us to rise to the occasion to fulfill a purpose (e.g. having to deal with a good friend's emergency), it may even be in conflict with our personal goals. It would be 'self'-ish to choose what is self-actualizing at such a juncture in our lives.

Young people who are learning about life and focused on their personal growth do need to self-actualize. They need to establish a profession and/or basic life skills for long-term viability, but they can still balance it as well with service to others, as we find in many high schools and colleges today.

Sometimes we find ourselves in a predicament whereby self-development is a must. Whether the result of scars from our past, addiction, abuse, or a variety of other conditions, we must focus on ourselves to fix what needs fixing and eventually be able to contribute to family or community.

The strategy in a life of purpose as an adult would be that when life calls on us to respond to situations and we need to develop our inner potential to rise to the occasion, then self-actualization is praiseworthy. In addition we might possess a hidden talent that can be trained to provide us with an income or a meaningful avocation that is also positive. But we don't have to actualize every talent/thought/desire we have just because it exists. We should self-actualize when it helps us fulfill our overall purpose, or to fulfill a specific purpose.

Since we are often easily swayed by our personal motivation, it is good to have a confidant who has our best interests in mind and can help us discern the right path.

6. There is a time and a place not to discuss purpose

Doing our part to "fix the world" does not mean that we need to police every shortcoming, mistake, or imperfection in the world. or in people around us. There is a time and place and a method to make our efforts fruitful and appreciated. Pointing out defects does not accomplish anything. The purpose is to fix or heal them, and it takes common sense to know when and how it can be done.

In addition, when others are in grief or great pain about a situation they find themselves in, they need us to show our compassion and love, not give them an explanation about how there is a purpose for what is happening to them. If they come to that conclusion on their own, it will help their healing, but to tell them so at their time of pain is insensitive. Once their pain subsides, then sharing thoughts about the purpose of why they are going through what they are experiencing can be helpful if communicated in a very sensitive manner.

Any effort to explain a purpose for tragedy, whether perpetrated by humankind or an act of God, is insensitive. In a life of purpose, we believe that somehow there is a purpose behind everything, even though our humanity cries out about injustice and questions how any purpose could possibly justify such events. Nevertheless, it could take decades before any reasonable guess about the purpose for these events comes to the surface.

7. Being prepared for unexpected changes in life

Every time we pass an oncoming car on the road, we are passing a stranger's circle of influence and doing our best not to collide. We all wear many hats and have our own influence on many concentric circles that surround us.

Sometimes we cross circles of influence that belong to strangers, and they can clash, as when we find ourselves in the wrong place at the wrong time; or complement each other, as when we make a new friend.

At times we are totally shocked to find that there was a short- or long-term influence on us that we were not aware of and we are perhaps repulsed by.

The lesson for a life of purpose is that while we may think that our lives are ours to lead, there are always changes going on around us, sometimes in concentric circles that we don't even know about, that can easily have an influence on our life.

In a life of purpose, we are aware that these outside influences could affect and change our life in small or large ways, either positively or negatively, at any time. We realize that as much as we may protect ourselves and our loved ones from any negative circles of influence, they can impact us as part of our purpose, and we stand prepared to try to deal with them should they come our way. We will not allow these surprises to derail us from our sense of purpose.

8. The role of entertainment and fun

While we are developing a life view that reflects a connection to purpose, sometimes our new value system can come into conflict with the society around us. Our society has done an excellent job of creating fun and enjoyment in our lives. We are provided with a plethora of professional entertainment, sports activities and online distractions. The list goes on and on with great ways to travel, spend our time and money, and be entertained.

In moderation there is no problem with any of these activities; to the contrary, the whole entertainment field can serve an important purpose to relax, inspire, enrich, educate, reenergize, and give us more strength and motivation to fulfill our purpose in life.

However, in a life of purpose, when fun and happiness become ends in themselves or consume more time and money than they should, we need to step away for a short time and ask ourselves what the real reason is for needing these outlets to such a great degree.

CHAPTER SIX

How Purpose Works - Creating Your Own Map

The paths of purpose discussed here apply potentially to every human being on the planet, rich or poor, healthy or sick, young or old.

Often circumstances push the development of one or more of these eight paths. At other times there is the luxury of choosing which path we want to focus on. During the course of a lifetime we could touch upon all eight to varying degrees, or just one.

Until now I have referred to the paths as spokes of a wheel, in which every path has the same importance. However, as we attempt to create our own map we each need to create a ladder with however many rungs we want to include, in whatever order we desire to take this journey.

Following is a general ladder which describes a journey which includes all eight paths and ascends rung by rung from the micro to the macro.

Step 1 - At the most basic level, survival and financial security are part of our base purpose.

Step 2 - We all have a purpose to procreate and raise our own biological or adopted children.

Step 3 - Improving our inner self and our attitudes is also an important endeavor in fulfilling a purpose. This path of inner change can take many directions.

Step 4 - Many of us have a drive to improve the conditions and circumstances of our life which directly affect us, our loved ones, and our surroundings.

Step 5 - We can find purpose in many events around us daily. Encounters with people, events we experience, and even the falling of a leaf, can all have a purpose on some level. This will be explained in greater depth in Chapter 9.

Step 6 - Mankind has been actively pursuing improvements in every aspect of life, as we are all wired in our core with an internal "DNA of purpose" to better the world at large for ourselves and for future generations.

Step 7 - For those of us who believe in a Higher Power that plays an active role in our life, a strong sense of purpose can infuse new energy into many aspects of our daily activity and/or religious observance.

Step 8 - The obstacles, conflicts, and tests in our lives also have purpose. It is important to know there is purpose in facing the specific challenges in our life. These challenges can occur in any of the other seven paths. Even dealing with all types of negativity has a purpose, as will be discussed at length in chapters 7 and 8.

Each one of these eight rungs on the ladder can uplift our daily life, create lasting happiness, and lead us in new and stimulating directions.

I list facing the tests of life as the highest rung, not because any of us should want to be tested, and not because I think it is the most important path, but rather because this rung represents the aspects of life which requires us to rise above our limitations in all the other seven paths. In many ways this is the most difficult path, but also one through which we can achieve great accomplishments.

Following are some examples of how these eight rungs can be experienced in our lives, corresponding to the eight steps listed above:

Step 1 - We should develop our potential to ensure our health and financial security. When our survival is being threatened, we must rise to the occasion to ensure our continuity, whether through financial, medical, or other ethical means. This path could come with great ease or great difficulty, depending on our circumstances and health.

Step 2 - Bringing a child into the world, or adopting, is a key priority, and every aspect of properly raising a child, from birth until full independence and on, also has a purpose.

Step 3 - Taking self-improvement seriously requires true introspection and growth, which can also lead to positive changes in our life, our relationships, and our personal happiness. This path includes the many varied efforts for self-actualization and self-development.

Step 4 - To improve our immediate surroundings we can get involved in community organizations, PTA, and charities or choose a job that aims to create positive local change (medicine, education, social work etc.). Many people feel a purpose in helping other people and expressing love, with the hope that they will make a positive difference in their lives.

Step 5 - Seeing purpose in the many events of our lives, both small and large, potentially gives them all new meaning. This can also be part of a spiritual path which helps create inner peace and happiness while renewing our ability to flow with the events of our life. We all need to be prepared to step up to the plate when circumstances call for us to do something positive.

Step 6 - Coming in touch with our core purpose can inspire us to become an active participant in making the world at large a better place. This could also be expressed through professional aspirations (research, politics, military service, or companies with a stated goal to make the world a better place etc.), charitable choices, voting preferences or personal pastimes.

Step 7 - Feeling the active presence of a Higher Power in life elevates a sense of purpose to new heights and infuses deeper meaning in every aspect of purpose. It also connects us to how our soul affects our destiny. The study of religious teachings can help motivate us to make our lives, and the world, a better place.

Step 8 - Coming to grips with the many challenges and negatives we inevitably face in life with a positive attitude is fulfilling a purpose in and of itself. Whether they are internal or external, confronting these challenges helps us change the world and fulfill our purpose in ways we would otherwise never attempt. We go out of our comfort zone and reveal our hidden potential.

When your energies are put into any of these or related purposeful efforts, whether you do it consciously for a purpose or not, you are aligned to some degree with your core purpose of changing the world for the better. Often you can feel in your gut the unique sense of fulfillment and happiness that comes as a result of connecting to a greater purpose in life.

Creating your own ladder in the beginning of your journey is important because it helps you prioritize now, so that in the future when you are faced with choices you will have your own personal guidelines to follow. When faced with difficult choices, it is usually best to choose to put your energies into a path that you assigned to a higher rung, as long as this will not cause new problems. Try to push yourself beyond your comfort zone to accomplish more than usual.

Try to include as many of the eight paths in your ladder to challenge yourself. Exploring each of the eight paths at some time can widen your horizons and potentially create new modes for fulfilling your purpose. We may have the potential to fulfill multiple purposes in a manner we could never imagine.

When, for whatever reason, your life is not feeling connected to purpose in a fulfilling way, it may be time to reappraise your ladder. As you grow and mature your life changes, as do your priorities and goals. The key is that you should be engaged in fulfilling your unique purpose in all its potential, wherever it may lead you.

Please remember as well that these eight paths of purpose are not the only paths of purpose in life. What makes them unique is that they are all based on the "operating system" of purpose, the DNA wired into your core being.

Many other belief systems espouse a purpose for mankind. I believe that their dependability, as well as their long-term success[13], are both dependent on how well aligned they are with this "operating system."

---

13   Perhaps the failure of communism as an economic system was partially because it was functioning in opposition to the DNA of purpose.

You should now be in a position to incorporate or expand purpose in your life to some degree.

> *There is no greater gift you can give or receive*
> *than to honor your calling. It's why you were*
> *born... and how you become most truly alive.*
> —OPRAH WINFREY

Let's take the next step and create your own personal map. Be prepared to write some notes to crystallize your map.

First of all, I recommend that you take an honest look at your life to better understand who you are, not only in your own eyes but also in the eyes of others. We need to take ownership of who we are and the effect we have on people, both positive and negative. Don't be surprised if you see or hear some things about your life that may be uplifting or disappointing. It could be you will even see something that others have told you in the past, but that you resisted. You may also see something so clearly about your life that you won't understand how it eluded you until now.

> *You will be your best self when you take time to*
> *understand what you really need, feel and want.*
> —DEBORAH DAY

During this process you may ask how does one find purpose in a negative event they experienced if they are filled with resentment and anger because of it? What does it take to detach oneself from old attitudes to accept new ones? How can a natural inner happiness develop if a person frequently feels like a victim?

These questions are just a few that you may need to ask when embarking on a life of purpose, depending on which path you choose to take.

It's a good idea to speak with a good friend, a confidante, or a therapist to make sure that your perception of yourself is an honest one. They are all part of your life for a reason, so ask one of them to join you for a cup of coffee and discuss some issues with them.

Once you make some progress, try to explore and even interpret some of the major and minor past events of your life.

These events will fall into three general categories (16):

1. those you clearly understand a purpose for
2. those you feel have a purpose but are not sure what their purpose actually is or was
3. those in which the purpose seems to be totally hidden from view

Here are some tips for putting a sense of purpose to work in each of these three categories:

1. People with short- or long-term challenges in survival, health, sustenance, or personal or family issues can realize with great clarity what they need to focus their lives on. The challenge may be to infuse a sense of purpose into daily activities related to those issues.

   Perhaps your present job, belief system, a new opportunity, or an extracurricular activity already gives you a deep sense of purpose. These are all very meaningful, and you may be ready to explore new paths of purpose you have not tried yet.

2. If nothing jumps out at you with clarity, examine the past and current stages and events of your life. Reflect on them until you have a taste of what purpose may be hidden to help it come to the surface. If an event in your life takes up a lot of space but has been given little attention, maybe there is a purpose there that you have not tapped into, as painful as it may be (no need to open a Pandora's Box for this exercise). If someone once complimented you for a talent you have but you never pursued it, it may be the time to look into it. You don't need to come to any conclusions, but do not be afraid to look at your whole package.

Even when you have a positive experience of déjà vu, a co-incidence, serendipity, or something that you feel was meant to happen, you can guess that there is some purpose behind that experience, but the challenge is that you don't know if this event is the beginning or the end of some ripple effect that has a long-term purpose or if it is related to something beyond your purview at this time. Thus it is usually not possible to come to any quick conclusions from one event. You can, however, heighten your sensitivity and see if other events lead you in a similar direction in the future. Ask a friend or confidant to help unravel some of the indicators you think are significant to create some order and direction out of them.

3. As explained in chapter 5, point #1, we don't always need to know what our purpose is. Nevertheless, we still need to live our life to the fullest, try our best to make the world a better place, and be confident that we are fulfilling a meaningful purpose. Our hope is that with time we will develop greater clarity and be able to act on that clarity to fulfill our individual purpose. Indeed, finding clarity is one of the greatest challenges, and benefits, of living a life of purpose, and it is ongoing.

Try to experiment with a life of purpose, and see how it gives a new view of both the daily and major events of your life. Take note of any out-of-the-ordinary events that happen during the day. Surely there are ways you can contribute to helping people and situations around you. Try to go out of your box, and even against your nature or nurture, and see where the situation leads you.

I believe you will be surprised, not only with the results, but also with the feeling you will sense as a result. Your positive actions may themselves help lead to clarity about your purpose as well.

Be careful, though. A life of purpose does not require trying to unravel the past or predict the future. It means living each day in a way that helps you develop your potential with all the tools you have today.

You may wonder at what pace you should try to apply the ideas in this book. This is a process that should not be rushed. One need not feel any obsession to all of a sudden try to see purpose in everything that happens. It needs to be a natural process of growth. It can be like opening a small gift every day and finding new surprises, because life itself takes on different packaging when we look at it through eyes of purpose.

To not overwhelm yourself, you may want to start in one relatively easy area of your life and work up to applying it to the more difficult areas of your life over the course of time.

Another approach would be to choose a chapter that resonated with you most, reread it, and then try to answer any of the questions listed at the end of this chapter as openly and honestly as possible. The exercises listed there are also meant to give you the opportunity to try to apply each chapter's ideas in some small way. Working on one question or exercise a week or month may be a healthy approach. After you finish, start applying your conclusions in some way.

Whatever method or pace you may use to develop the ideas in this book, let your core sense of purpose come gently to the surface, and see whether you feel more personally fulfilled as a result.

You may have to wait for the opportunity to arise. It will be totally unpredictable as to when, where, and how you will feel it, but when you do, you will know it is your turn to step forward.

If possible, dip your big toe in and see how it feels. If it requires a big commitment, use your intellect, emotions, and intuition to choose the right path to follow. If possible don't take on the harder challenges until you feel confident, unless a particular situation demands your attention. Slowly but surely you can take on more and more until leading a purposeful life becomes a natural and uplifting part of your day.

Be confident that with the tools you are now familiar with, you can apply the principles of purpose to whatever large or small part of your life you wish to apply them to.

Once we live life with this sense of purpose, we face each new day with enthusiasm. Every encounter takes on meaning and is unique. We can be the masters of our attitude as we tap into our inner resources in a way that frees us from the natural boundaries of a life full of predictable behaviors. We can sit at the center of a circle from where we see a new view on our life within a bigger context. We can live life with meaning, inspiration, and an inner compass that guides us along a path that puts the dichotomies of life into perspective.

It may require much effort and hard work at times, but the end result makes it well worth going through the process.

Following are questions to ponder, and exercises to try, for the introduction and chapters one through four:

Introduction - The Paradox of Purpose

1. Do you feel an inner desire to connect to your purpose in life? Do you want to connect to it? Explain.

2. Do you resist feeling that your life has purpose? If so, is it coming from your head or your heart? Are you afraid? Why?

Exercise

1. Take one event in your life, good or bad, and think of a purpose for why you had to go through that experience.

Chapter 1 - Changing the World

1. In what ways have you felt a sense of inner satisfaction in the past when you made your world a better place to live?

2. Do you agree there are limitations in fulfilling a purpose that is focused on self-actualization?

Exercise

1. Pick an area of your life in which you can do more to change the world for the better. Do a few things in that area and then write your thoughts and feelings about any sense of fulfillment you get from it.

Chapter 2 - To Everything a Purpose

1. Do you relate to the idea that you are a unique person, unlike any other, with a special contribution to make to the world? If not, why not? Explain.

2. Do you sometimes feel like a victim of life and circumstances? Explain.

3. What special contribution do you make to your family, friends, and community? What more could you do?

4. What talents do you have that you know have not yet really developed?

5. What blemishes does your personality have that you could make more of an effort to correct? Do you see a purpose in improving them?

Exercises

1. Try to see yourself as others see you. Which positive attribute of yours would they encourage you to develop? Which negative one should you better control? Don't hesitate to ask somebody for help in this exercise. You may be surprised at what you hear.

Chapter 3 – The Path of Inner Change

1. Which of the four paths of inner change do you think you need to work on most? How can you do that?

2. How can you make your relationships more purpose-based?

3   Can you think of one area of ethics that you would like to improve upon to be more aligned with fulfilling your purpose?

4. Do you feel in your heart of hearts that the "pursuit of happiness" can often be frustrating and sometimes quite costly (not just financially)?

Exercises

1. For a full week, in a situation when you would normally be unhappy, choose to be happy and record how it feels.

2. Pick one other behavior from any of the other three paths and try to make a positive change in your normal knee-jerk reactions.

3. Try to define for yourself the difference between regular happiness and inner fulfillment you feel when you fulfill a purpose during your day.

Chapter Four – Was It Meant to Be?

1. Have you ever felt a special sense of clarity why something was happening to you?

2. Are you open to seeing a spiritual dimension to events in your life? Does that help you see purpose in your life?

3. How does a belief in a Higher Power affect your sense of purpose? Does it inspire you to accomplish more in your life?

Exercise

1. Try to react to any future event in your life from both a non-spiritual and a spiritual perspective. Do you notice differences in how you react?

In conclusion, life is a deep mystery, but it is also a journey we must take, and part of our challenge is to gather as many tools that we can. These tools can come in many forms, and ideally we can internalize as many as we need to fulfill the journey to its greatest potential.

I do hope that the first part of this book has provided you with some tools that will help you better fulfill your purpose in life. If you have even a bit of greater clarity about purpose than you did when you started the book, please continue to read Part II, which can take your sense of purpose to a whole new level. You will gain many more tools and find interesting answers to the following questions, within the context of a purpose based life:

1. Why are we not born with an awareness of our purpose?

2. What is the difference between knee-jerk reactions, decisions and choices?

3. How do willpower, choice and purpose work together?

4. Why are some choices so incredibly difficult?

5. Why do bad things happen to good people?

6. What is a simple system that provides daily clarity in a life of purpose?

PART II
Purpose 201

CHAPTER SEVEN
Making the Hard Choices

I have divided this chapter into two sections, since the topic has so many interesting angles that need to be well digested. Section II of this chapter also serves as an introduction to chapter eight.

As we try to develop sensitivity to our inner purpose, certain skills need to be fine-tuned and others need to be learned. One important skill we can use in all eight paths is our ability to make choices.

Without this tool we are not able to adapt fully to the changing circumstances around and within us. Our ability to live a full life of purpose in any of the paths would be compromised.

The dynamics of choice are often misunderstood and so it is a talent which is usually underused. Most of us need to better activate, develop, and strengthen our willpower to make choices and follow through on them. As life changes and new circumstances present themselves, we need to be ready to make the choices that help us fulfill our evolving purpose.

For choices to accomplish a purpose, they require the willpower to bring them to fruition. Willpower is the gas that fuels the choice mechanism we have. The harder the choice, the more willpower is needed.

Choice and willpower work as a team. Choice by itself is ineffective, as many of our New Year's resolutions prove. Willpower without wise choices can be misdirected and go in many negative directions, as we see from people who have a strong will but no self-control.

In a life of purpose our *choices* should direct the *willpower* to fulfill a positive *purpose*.

But this is not like a relay team where the choice is made once and then the baton is given over to willpower to carry it to the finish line. The "choice" to drive our willpower has to be an ongoing force, not to be interrupted. Choice provides the motivation for the willpower to generate its unique energy. The struggle to choose goes on. It's not enough to make a choice once and assume it will get done as chosen.

If we live without making real choices, we are living on autopilot. We see this phenomenon in religion, in marriage, in jobs, and in many relationships. If we are not actively choosing to be present in our endeavors, we can start doing things by rote. If we are not consciously choosing to connect to our spouse or loved ones, we can drift apart.

The key to success is realizing that choices can be made daily, sometimes many times a day, and we must strive to keep our willpower motivated so the momentum continues.

Choice is the silent mechanism for fulfilling our purpose. It is more than just a tool. It is a partner. Choice, willpower, and the DNA of purpose are all dormant forces within us that are waiting to be activated.

Unfortunately free choice is a bit of a mystery and hard to define.

We have no choice as to our body, our relatives, or the society we live in. Psychologists tell us that 95 percent of our personality is shaped by the time we are five years old—very little choice there!

In addition, we all make many important "decisions" that can change our lives and the lives of many people around us. We can even fulfill an important purpose in this manner. But decisions, as important as they may be, are usually heavily influenced by our nature or nurture—our genetics or our environment/upbringing. There is nothing wrong with this fact; it's just not a real choice.

"Choices" that are heavily influenced by knee-jerk reactions, personality traits, culture, our DNA map, or natural instincts are really more like decisions than choices. When we "choose" between a pecan pie and lemon chiffon, it is usually our taste buds that are "making the decision" for us. It's also not really a choice.

Even most objective decisions that we make are simply based on our past experiences, our qualities and weaknesses, our comfort level, or simply a good look at information available to us at the time. We act on this basis day in and day out.

When we choose a college, a house, a spouse, a career, is it really us who are choosing, or are the circumstances of our life nudging us along in that direction?

Even when we make some moral and ethical choices, is it free choice, or is it because of our upbringing and social and/or religious influences?

To make it even more difficult to figure out, choice seems to be filled with danger. Throughout the history of humankind, we have witnessed too many people "choosing" to destroy rather than build. Humans are the only beings who can "choose" to exploit our environment, abuse others, or wreak havoc in society. We sometimes "choose" to use technology, sexuality, money, or drugs to ruin lives, including our own.

The question therefore is how and when do we actually make free choices in our life, especially when the influences of our nature and nurture have such control over us and our decisions?

Let's try to answer this question by looking at two situations I would say involved real free choice.

Amanda came from a poor family and worked hard to climb the corporate ladder, with great success. Unfortunately the higher she climbed, the more dependent on drugs she became. Her husband wanted her to go for counseling, but she refused, feeling like nothing could stop her. The issue almost came to a quick stop when her habit was discovered at work. At that moment she realized for the first time in her life that her aspirations for success were motivated by negative intentions that came from deep within. She was chasing success at any cost and was using drugs to numb the guilt and uneasiness she felt inside. She knew she would either get fired or have to be totally open and ask for some time off. The latter choice was totally against her nature, but she did it and got some intense help, which required many tough choices as well. Eventually she went back as a new person to a successful career that lasted for years.

Rick was a high school football player with what seemed to be a great future. He was well liked and had better-than-average grades. He didn't have to work too hard at what he did. His parents thought he had much greater potential and tried in their own way to prod him onward, but to no avail. His girlfriend was happy with him the way he was, which was fine with him. She had a tremendous influence on him and was codependent as well. His parents were aware of the codependency, but there was little they could do. The first time Rick really had to dig deep and make an important decision in his life was when it came to choosing a college. He was accepted with a football scholarship to a good school, but his girlfriend wanted him to be in the town where she was going to school. It took a lot of soul searching, resisting strong pressure, and taking a long look at his future before he decided, with his parents' guidance, that he had to cut off the relationship with his girlfriend. It was the hardest choice of his life. He went on to excel in college and football, and he met a new girlfriend without a problem.

Circumstances forced Amanda and Rick to dig deep within themselves when confronted with having to choose the life they wanted to live. They faced life crises that made them aware that choice was not a luxury; it was a necessity. They had to take a crash course on how to make tough choices in life, perhaps for the first time ever.

Do we all have to wait until life pushes us against the wall before we make such choices? Is free choice reserved only for when we face a major dilemma, as in the case of Amanda and Rick?

The answer is a resounding no! We have real choices every day in what we think about, how we speak, and what we do. We don't always have to behave with knee-jerk reactions or preconditioned mediocrity. We do have a unique ability to choose to go beyond the limits of our nature and nurture and make personal choices on an ongoing basis. We can learn from Amanda and Rick how to do it.

We can *choose* how to react to a hurtful experience. We can *choose* to be there for a friend in a vulnerable situation. We can *choose* to replace negative thought patterns with positive ones.

In a life of purpose, one of the ways we can regularly make real choices is to stretch (or bend) ourselves in some positive way or resist our natural urge for some negative action.

Let's read that statement again and let it sink in.

Our nature and nurture would have us take one path, but in a life of purpose, we rise above them, or go against them, to choose a different, better path.

In a life of purpose we choose to activate our willpower on an ongoing basis, not just when we have to.

By definition, most of us have limited opportunities during the day to fix and refine the world around us, but we can always fix and improve our inner deficiencies and weaknesses. These are often the most diffi-cult challenges that we need to rectify to make this a better world. This applies whether we have many external challenges in life, or few if any.

Bettering ourselves is a lifelong struggle in which we can practice mak-ing good choices even in the small details of our life. When we are faced with two foods we like and we choose the healthier one, even though we like the other one's taste better, that decision is exercising free choice. When we hold back from giving unwarranted criticism even though our nature is to be critical, that is rising above our limita-tions. If we have an addictive personality and we resist our weakness, that feat is real choice. When we decide to do what we believe is right, even when others might scoff or we may suffer monetary loss, we are also exercising choice. If we are stingy by nature but act generously when the situation calls for it, we are subduing our nature and choos-ing a better path.

In this area of life, healthy paths for self-actualization can be helpful.

Inroads in psychology and psychiatry over the past one hundred years have helped liberate millions of people who were held hostage to character disorders and mental illness. The self-help industry provides unprecedented tools for personal growth and inner peace. We have changed our understanding of life from a road with many bumps to one that is a ladder to climb.

As individuals, though, we still have great difficulty choosing to do the right thing or say the right words. In a certain sense, the improvements we can make in fields such as education, technology, politics, business, medicine, and science are easy, compared to inner challenges. In those fields we can build on the shoulders of all the great people of the past who blazed the trail for us, using our innate talents and intelligence to take their work and accomplishments to the next step.

In our personal lives, however, we are sometimes faced with choices that make us feel like we are starting from scratch. We may have received the benefits of learning from moral and ethical behavior around us, but we do not inherit the wisdom, self-control, and inner strength of those who preceded us. Each of us has to learn these skills ourselves. Unfortunately, I have not seen any courses on how to activate choice and willpower.

Each of us has to learn on our own how to make good choices and activate our willpower. The struggle from within does not necessarily get easier with time and even a strong moral base doesn't protect us from our inherent or adapted weaknesses.

We could be a genius with high morals and great solutions, but if our treasure of hidden willpower is not developed, our ability to choose can remain ineffective for an entire lifetime, and we will not be able to choose a better life for ourselves and our loved ones.

Sometimes we don't even "choose" the wrong path; we just end up there by default, since we fall back to knee-jerk instincts. This situation could be because of any of the following reasons:

- Laziness
- Lack of self-confidence
- Self-doubt
- Indecisiveness
- Insecurity
- Social pressures
- Fears
- Anger
- Selfishness
- Lack of self-awareness

Any of these tendencies can incapacitate our ability to choose and undermine our innate ability to live a life of purpose. In addition, our pursuit of, or attraction to different forms of pleasure creates strong deterrents to making clear-headed choices.

Choice is a uniquely human trait that gives each of us great potential to accomplish something purposeful every day of our lives. The opportunities choice provides us with should never be underestimated.

Only we human beings have the ability to rise to this challenge—to push ourselves to break free of our natural limits and our knee-jerk reactions.

When we do not exercise the uniquely human gift of choice, we short-change ourselves and those around us. We are ignoring one of our greatest innate skills as human beings.

Near the end of the book of Deuteronomy in the Bible, it is stated, "I have set before you a choice of life or death, blessing or curse. You should choose life!" (17) The Bible does not need to tell us to choose life as opposed to death—we all know that choice instinctively. What the passage is telling us is that *we should choose to live every moment using our ability to make choices.* We don't have to accept our own inner status quo. We should live our lives in a way of always choosing. (18)

What does personal choice have to do with 'making the world a better place for future generations'? Simple! As mentioned before, every one of us is an important part of the world, and fixing ourselves is just as important as—and probably more difficult than—fixing the world at large.

In addition, to change anything in the world around us, our accomplishments would always be limited if we were not able to go beyond our own limits when the situation called for it.

If we can't go beyond our own nature and nurture, not only would we not be able to fix ourselves, we would be limited by our self. Similarly, our ability to influence our environment, and pass our many tests in life, would be predictable and limited as well.

If I can't stretch or change myself to adapt to new challenges, how prepared am I to fix the world around me or deal with the roller coaster that life can sometimes become? If we naturally take the comfortable or easy way out by letting our nature and nurture control our lives, instead of aspiring to be the best person we can be, it would be hard to change the world around us effectively.

We may be wonderful and talented people, even successful in most everything we do, but if we take the easy way out all the time, we would be limited in fulfilling our purpose when an opportunity or challenge arose. On the other hand, when we learn to go beyond our nature and nurture, we are better equipped to fix the world within and around us.

Joe and Heather had two healthy children. After a few years, Heather started urging her husband to have another child. Joe was perfectly happy with the status quo. He was not excited but knew once Heather got this goal into her mind, it was going to happen. It was not as easy as they expected, but finally she became pregnant, and when the baby was born, he had Down syndrome. Joe was devastated, but Heather was ready for the rough road ahead and knew she would have to do a lot of hand-holding for Joe to get through the new challenges. It was an uphill battle for years, and Joe had a combination of anger, resentment, and disappointment. As the years went by he saw Heather and little Kent blossom together, and he realized that he was living a life focused on finding escapes to reach happiness, but he was out of touch with his reality. All he had to do was finally make a choice to refocus his life from the reality he wanted to the reality he had. It took tremendous inner willpower, but when he finally did it and became a loving father to Kent, life and their marriage changed for the better.

Most of the people who made significant changes in their communities and in the world did so by pushing themselves and going beyond their nature. When we succeed and actually do change our inner world in some small way, it leads to bigger changes in the world at large. Fulfilling our purpose on the inside leads to fulfilling our purpose on the outside.

Few people are born natural leaders. Managers can make good decisions, but leaders go beyond their nature. Leaders, and especially the great ones, have to grow into their positions by learning from mistakes, recovering from failures, and overcoming many obstacles, both from within and without. They specialize in rising above their limitations and as a result change the course of history.

In a life of purpose, activating our willpower to support our ability to choose is one of the highest goals we can attain. Once we learn how to choose to go beyond our nature and nurture, we begin to understand how limiting our nature and nurture truly are.

Once in a while I ask people to try the following experiment: One time during each of the next four weeks, exercise this type of choice in your life. I make it clear that "going the extra mile" does not mean just doing a little extra; it means pushing ourselves beyond our normal behavior in some small or large way. At first it is difficult, but with time it gets easier. Almost always people report back to me that as hard as it was, they felt a great sense of inner accomplishment.

When our spouses, children, parents, bosses, or employees see that we are tapping into our willpower to go beyond our normal mode of behavior, we make a much greater impression than we can imagine. Families are transformed when one member strives to be a recovering addict or rises to face a great personal challenge.

Sometimes people come to me with a problem that requires the change of a major behavior pattern. Before I work on their issue, I first may have to see whether they can activate their willpower to choose and develop their inner talent in a smaller challenge. Once they taste the sweet smell of victory when they reach beyond their natural limits in some small issue they face, then we can talk about changing the bigger issues they first came for.

The goal is to develop this skill so that we apply it not only when we are under pressure or when others expect us to rise to the occasion, but also whenever we are faced with a difficult decision. The same will that drives us to reach an occasional goal against all odds should also be applied to our daily life to some degree to help us overcome challenges and reach dreams that we never thought were within our reach.

In conclusion, the fact is that our choices can have immense impact on the world far beyond our immediate circles. We have the opportunity and responsibility to choose to be major players in the process of making the world a better place.

By nature of the fact that we are alive, we all have the potential to choose to live in a new and better way, to rise above our natural behaviors, and connect to a place deep within that gives us the peace and happiness we all crave.

Remember, every situation presents us with the potential to accomplish something personal that was never accomplished before in the history of humankind. We can take advantage of the opportunity with a purposeful attitude, or we can potentially lose the opportunity. The choice is ours, and it's a choice we may be able to make many times a day.

The ripple effect of our choices never ends, which is why it is important to make choices in line with the DNA of purpose.

So now let's work together to make the world, and ourselves, better than when we came into it.

SECTION II

A major question still beckons. If we try to fulfill our purpose and make some meaningful choices when we "fix" something in ourselves or in our sphere of influence, why does it have to be so difficult, and at times actually painful? Why is choice so challenging? Why are some choices of right and wrong so hard to make and then fulfill?

Why is it that a teenager who has kleptomania and a parent who wants to control his or her anger can both feel overwhelmed by their challenges? Why do addicts struggle to succeed in recovery, or criminals who sincerely want to change their lives have such a hard time doing so?

I struggled with these questions, and didn't find a solid answer until I came across a 1,500-year-old commentary from a great sage about a sentence in the book of Genesis. At first it seemed strange, but the more I thought about it, the more it resolved many questions I had.

It is written that after the world was created, God said that it was "very good. (19)" The sage asks why it was very good, as opposed to just good. The surprising answer that he gives is that the word *good* refers to Adam and Eve's inclination to do good, and the *very* of *very good* refers to their propensity to do bad (20). In other words, this internal struggle of both human inclinations is the way life was meant to be, and it is the propensity for bad that makes the whole of creation *very* good.

How can it be that both inclinations together—to do good and bad— are called *very good?* What kind of system is it that creates such duality and causes so many inner conflicts?

The only answer I could find that matches the reality of the life we all live is that the strong pull of the negative has to be powerful enough to provide real choices in life. Only this way can we make hard choices and truly have free choice.

If making the right choice came, *in any way*, as a result of going with the flow, what achievement would that be? If negative influences were weaker, the good would naturally prevail. If we always felt a stronger pull to do good in our lives and rarely faced life's negatives, our freedom of choice would be seriously compromised. Life's purpose would be missing a crucial ingredient.

Let's take an even deeper look at another harsh aspect of the balance between positive and negative. Most of us see, and many have actually experienced, how at times the pull of the negative has an unfair advantage over the positive. It is often easier and more appealing to do bad than to do good, to criticize than to praise, and to destroy rather than to build. We see how easy it is to hurt another's feelings or give a child an unforgettable emotional scar. One act of deception can undermine years of trust; one misdeed can ruin a sterling career.

The power of the negative is at times able to wield a bat that is much stronger than a wand of good. (21)

This disproportionate balance can create some challenging circumstances for us. The reason for this imbalance is because real "choosing" must sometimes involve overcoming powerful internal obstacles and/or strong negative external influences, wherein the balance is tipped heavily toward the negative.

This is the ultimate "free choice." Choosing "good" must sometimes be a willful choice even against great odds. These situations give us the opportunity, as few events in life do, to find out about our inner core being and what we are made of.

So the creation is called "very good" because the bad and the negative can often have a stronger pull, such that we have to go beyond or even against our nature in order to *choose* "good." That good then rises to the definition of being "*very* good."

This reality also explains why when we learn from our mistakes the lessons last longer; why light which comes from darkness seems much brighter; why the triumph of good over bad is so valued, and why victory after defeat tastes so much better. It also explains why Amanda's recovery and successful career meant so much to her and her family. It was 'very good'.

Now we can understand the paradox of purpose mentioned in the book introduction. The paradox was why humans, the crown of creation, are the only members of the universe that do not naturally fulfill their purpose?

Now it seems clear that if we were born with the instinctive knowledge of our purpose, it would undermine our personal ability to *choose* to fulfill that purpose. There would be no such thing as real choice. There would be no 'good' that qualifies to be *very* good. The paradox of purpose is real!

The occasional imbalance of excessive negativity provides another important insight into the nature of life itself. It can help us understand why our good deeds seem to be so fragile in the face of negativity or even evil. It prepares us not to be surprised that negativity may reside just beneath the surface and can easily appear in any situation we may face. It also gives us an idea why it is so difficult sometimes to choose to do the right thing and fulfill a worthwhile purpose.

More importantly, it provides us with needed tools to tackle the question of why bad things happen to good people, as we will explore in the next chapter.

Questions and Exercises

1. How many of the obstacles on page 100 are issues you have to deal with? Why do some stand out more than others? What can you do to overcome them?

2. Do you live mostly by relying on knee-jerk reactions, making decisions, or exercising free choice? Give examples.

3. Can you think of ways to increase your willpower to better power your free choice?

4. In what areas of your life do you feel you can choose to be a better person?

5. Think of a time when you went beyond your nature and nurture by bending or resisting your natural inclination. How did it feel? Would you do it again?

Exercise

1. Pick a minor area in your life that you know you need to change or that your family would like you to change and resolve at least once in each of the next four weeks to go against your nature to change it. Make notes of how you, and they, react.

CHAPTER EIGHT
Why Good and Bad Happen to Everyone

*J*ust as it is important to understand why choice is an important tool to enhance fulfillment of our purpose, it is also important to understand the most powerful obstacle to fulfilling our purpose, one which has the power to totally distract us in all eight paths.

When we face deep hurt, suffering, corruption, and/or wanton destruction, our connection to purpose can easily be brought to its knees. Serious tests and obstacles in life can totally derail us from fulfilling our purpose, especially when we see ourselves as good people trying to choose to do the right things in life.

This is why fine-tuning the eighth rung of the purpose ladder, and developing the purpose based attitudes needed to face life's tests, is so important.

The fact is that when we react to life's challenges, like discomfort (give me a break), injustice (this is not fair), pain (ouch!), tragedy (why me?), evil (how can you do this?), or even death (OMG!), we have a choice to react by going in one of two general directions. We can be their long-term victims (victim mode), or we can try our best to adjust over time and then flow with the new reality (flow mode) and become stronger people because of them.

The latter is a hard choice, as Chaya and I learned after both the birth and death of our son, but it is not beyond our reach. In a life of purpose, the challenge is not just to ride the waves of our tough chapters in life and then run back to the status quo. The challenge is to "stretch the bungee cord" to see and experience the negatives as part of our purpose as well. We need solid tools if we are to rise to the occasion and react with fortitude and resolve, or else we can lose sight of our purpose and potentially be overtaken by the power of the negative events around us.

Joanne had been divorced for seven years and was still struggling to make ends meet. Her ex, on the other hand, was financially secure and had soon remarried. She was full of resentment but eventually made peace with her situation, until she was laid off from her job. Things went from bad to worse, until eventually she was evicted from her apartment. Her out-of-town sister offered to take her in, but it would mean leaving her grown—but still single—children behind. She was at the end of her rope, when it occurred to her that maybe there was a purpose behind all this: perhaps she should move to a new locale for the next stage of her life. With this painful realization, she shared her plans with her children and made the move to her sister's house with uncharacteristic courage and determination. A simple change in attitude transformed her life.

Everybody has a unique purpose in this life, and there are no guarantees that your purpose does not include some real tests in life. In addition, regardless of how "good" or "bad" a person you are, you still have to make choices in life and take the risks that come with those choices as well. The script of your life is not limited to the exposures you would like to limit it to.

"Bad" things that are totally out of our control and not of our making (e.g. acts of God) can happen to anybody. You don't need to be a rocket scientist to realize that being good does not create a protective wall around you. You can be the nicest person in the world, but no religion or insurance policy in the world is going to protect you from life's vicissitudes.

We also know that good and bad things happen to both good and bad people. There seems to be no rhyme or reason to how this phenomenon works. We don't question *that* bad things do happen to good people; instead we ask *why* do bad things happen to good people?

Let's try to understand the question by finding a better definition for *good* and *bad*.

We can rightly describe an event as "painful," "tragic," "heart wrenching," and so on, but when you stop to think about it, describing something as simply "bad" or "good" is a human value judgment, not a description of reality. What may be bad to one may seem good to another or may even be viewed by the same person differently under different circumstances at different times.

The unhappy wife who dreaded an upcoming divorce now lives happily with a caring second husband and would never look back. The man who knew his jail sentence was unjust then turned his life around while there. The ten-year-old child who spent three months in the hospital was inspired to become a doctor as a direct result. The parent who cried for months about a recently diagnosed autistic son eventually grew to love and cherish his uniqueness.

Joe was suing his local youth center because his son broke his leg during summer camp. The unfortunate event ruined the summer for the family and caused great pain to his son. On September 12, 2001, he dropped his lawsuit. He had to take his son to an early-morning doctor's appointment the day before and thus became one of the few employees of Cantor Fitzgerald in the World Trade Center who was spared from the terrorist attack.

Nobody can claim that such experiences were not painful at the time they happened, but what appears to be bad today may be seen as good tomorrow or next year or ten years from now, once the hourglass of purpose has had time to fill.

In general, we live in a society where the 'normative' definition of *good* is happy, beautiful, fun, healthy, and successful. *Bad* is defined as their absence or the opposite—pain, poverty, loneliness, illness, evil, depression, anger, etc. These are very human definitions that we quickly ascribe to situations and people. Sometimes these descriptions are given as a knee-jerk reaction.

In a life of purpose, however, good and bad are labels that should be used sparingly.

The details of our life present us with many types of circumstances. We would all like for each of these circumstances to match up perfectly with the 'normative' definition of *good*, in which case life would be ideal. Unfortunately, as we all know only too well, that doesn't always happen.

When we face that gap between the "good" circumstances of life that we desire and the ones that we end up with (which may seem "bad"), we feel challenged or even cheated. Based on normative definitions of *good* and *bad*, we may feel a sense of injustice and anger when faced with this gap.

> Suzanne shared with her therapist the many problems she had and why she was totally overwhelmed. She told him "this is not the life I planned for". He asked her to tell him all the good things in her life that she also planned for. She had to stop and think but was able to come up with a nice list. When they compared all the 'good' to the 'bad' she felt somewhat relieved that her life was not totally out of control, and left with a plan how to internally handle the 'gap'.

However, once we give a purpose-based definition of *good* and *bad*, the gap doesn't look the same.

In a life of purpose, something is "good" if it helps us fulfill our purpose, and it is "bad" if it hinders the fulfillment of our purpose.

In other words, in a life of purpose there is no gap, because we are not using normative knee-jerk definitions of *good* and *bad* to describe events that happen to us. We are using purpose-based definitions.

In the face of our challenges we need to rise beyond our nature and nurture to *choose* our reaction and attitude. It is too easy to use our default reaction to call something bad and feel like a victim. It is a very human response, but it is not a purposeful response.

A purposeful reaction does not mean that we have mastered our emotions. It does not mean that we won't be devastated by something that happens to us. It does mean that as time goes on we are open to try to pick up the pieces and eventually change our view of the "bad" event. With much effort we strive to stay focused on the aspect of the event which happened for a good purpose.

As hard as it is to think of this when we are actually going through the "bad," the fact is that transforming an experience from "bad" to "good" has been accomplished over and over again by millions of people over time. How many books and movies highlight this very human feat?

> *The climb might be tough and challenging, but the view is worth it. There is a purpose for that pain; you just can't always see it right away.*
> —Victoria Arlen

From this perspective, even pain and suffering can have a good purpose.

Pain is considered terrible if it is the result of an accident or if we see it as unjustified. On the other hand, we understand why a woman has to experience labor pain, and we know the path to healing, recovery, and victory can involve pain. In these cases we recognize pain can serve a good purpose, and we accept it as a necessary part of life. Although we are not capable of understanding how other types of pain and suffering can be good, in the dimension of purpose, we accept that they also can serve a good ultimate purpose.

When a white blouse has a small stain, we put it through the washing machine. If the stain comes out, we then put it in the dryer and then iron it at seven hundred degrees. If that blouse had feelings, it would rightfully see us as cruel and unreasonable for responding to a small stain with such vehemence. But the owner's intention was only to improve the condition of the blouse and return it to its original beauty, not to cause pain.

Along this same line of thought, when people experience numerous problems one after another, it is not simply that they are victims of bad luck, but rather it is an indication that they have much to accomplish in their purpose and tremendous inner potential to reveal.

Elisa and Dave had a great life together. They appeared to have it all until the recession hit, and then Dave's business went spiraling out of control. Payroll became a monthly nightmare, and he could not meet his financial obligations. The couple was not prepared for the stress their financial situation put on their marriage. Fortunately through tremendous perseverance and some good fortune, Dave was able to stabilize his business. He could finally breathe freely for the first time in a year. Two days after his first worry-free payroll, his teenage son was in a serious car accident. He met his wife at the hospital, and when they realized how serious his condition was, they cried. He asked his wife, "Why is all this happening to us, one punch following the other?" Elisa's response shocked him but also saved him from a meltdown. She told him that she had asked herself the same question, and this was her answer: the struggle they went through financially was the much-needed preparation for what they were about to experience. She told him she was confident that they now had the tools to get through this new challenge as well.

It is not just a matter of seeing the glass half full. It is a matter of seeing purpose behind all the changes in our lives and accepting them as challenges of great importance.

You don't have problems. You have challenges.
–RABBI M. M. SCHNEERSON

In a life of purpose it may take years or decades before the ripple effect of change reveals the good hidden within an event, but its purpose is the eventual improvement of some aspect of our lives or the world itself.

As hard as it is for me to write the following three paragraphs, in the dimension of purpose, even when facing death, we can be sure we are encountering an unshakable truth. Death is the ultimate statement that one's purpose in this world has been completed. There is no more fixing to be done. The day before Boruch died, he asked my wife what death was, and she answered, "It is simply moving through a door from one room into another."

Whether a person's passing is gradual or sudden, there is meaning behind it, as well as in the timing of it. Whether natural or caused by a doctor's error, a car accident, or a murderer's gun, death has a deep purpose beneath the surface. We are simply not privy to it. The ripple effect of that death, and the life that preceded it, continues in ways we cannot even imagine.

Those of us who believe that things do happen for a purpose accept that tragedies don't happen at random. They are painful turning points pushing us into the next chapter of our lives, all necessary for fulfilling our unique purpose. These events become an integral part of our new identity, not a contradiction to it. It is OK if life will never be the same. We will build on our past to make the future better.

"Pain is human; suffering is optional" is a saying I saw on a bulletin board at the local community center soon after Boruch passed away. For my wife and me, the pain of our loss is still there and our tears are just beneath the surface, but many years of healing, our growing family, and exploring our sense of purpose have all helped dissipate the suffering.

When Boruch was born I asked, "Why us?" By the time he died, as emotionally devastated as I was, I realized there was no reason to ask the question. We don't need all the answers—we are not going to get them anyway. *In a life of purpose, we don't look at life as being out of control. Neither do we see it as something that we have to control.* We just have to be ready to 'stretch our bungee cord' to adjust to a new life plan if it becomes necessary to do so. We have to be prepared for life's changes, whatever they may be.

I hope and pray that we should have no more tragedies in our lives and ask God every day not to test us, although I do feel more prepared for life's ups and downs than ever before. With that said, I also know only too well how vulnerable I am and how little I understand.

In the 1800s a European rabbi inherited a lucrative lumber business and a large forest. He hired managers to run his business and dedicated himself to teaching. One day his students heard that his forest had burned down and were wary of breaking the news to him. They decided that his top student would engage him in a discussion about the Talmudic passage, "Just as we make a blessing for the good, so we should make a blessing for the bad." (22) After listening for an hour to his teacher brilliantly expounding on the verse, the student broke the tragic news to him. The rabbi fainted. When he came to, he noted his student's disappointment in his reaction and said, "I realize now that I really do not understand the Talmudic passage."

There are no guarantees that anyone will be spared one or more tragedies during a lifetime, and none of us know what we have to go through to fulfill our life's purpose. We do know that there is much imperfection in this world. No one is immune from it, and as much as we may try to avoid it, we are all bound to encounter it to some degree. The question is how we are going to react to it.

Based on all of the above, bad things do happen to good people all the time, but good people are not being unfairly picked on, because "bad" happens to everyone—for a purpose.

In summary, staying connected to purpose when we are the victim of a health situation, accident, abusive relationship, act of God, crime, or wonton negligence is the most difficult part of living a life of purpose.

We wonder what purpose could there possibly be for what we are enduring.

Our emphasis on needing to describe people or events as good or bad distracts us and potentially prevents us from fulfilling our purpose in dealing with them properly. Similarly, getting absorbed with assigning blame for our situation only distracts us from focusing on getting through our crisis. This does not mean that in certain situations we should not pursue justice. It does mean that our focus needs to be on surviving as best as possible and accepting that on some level there is a purpose for the experience. Negative events in our lives do not excuse us from our responsibility to do our part in making the world a better place.

Every event in our life is part of the hourglass working toward the fulfillment of our individual purpose. Maybe eventually we will understand it to be true, and maybe not. However, being negative or a victim or spending our time and energy trying to justify or give a reason to such events or asking "why me?" all serve no positive purpose for getting us back to living life to its fullest.

With the understanding of how purpose thinks, how purpose works, and how we can walk through life with purpose, we are better able to make our lives more meaningful and balanced. We can find purpose and happiness even in the midst of life's imperfections and even in the face of its greatest challenges.

Equipped with this knowledge, we won't be caught off guard in case of adversity, and we can attain a fulfilling life of purpose no matter what comes our way.

Questions and Exercises

1. Can you think of "bad" events in your life that turned out to have a "good" purpose?

2. What do you have to do to be at peace with the most painful moments and scars of your life and to accept that they had an important purpose that you had to experience?

3. Can you accept that the bad events were not accidents, but that many steps were involved in making them happen the way they did?

Exercise

1. Write a one-page list of all the major events of your life in three columns. In the first column list the event. In the second, list whether it seemed to be good or bad at the time it happened, and in the third column list whether it was "good" or "bad" in purpose terms. Does the purpose column give a new perspective on your life?

CHAPTER NINE
Living in 3-P

*T*he path of seeing many of the events in our daily life as opportunities for change was introduced in chapter 4. As described there, it can be viewed as a practical path to change our surroundings and/or a spiritual path to see purpose in events that happen to us. Either way, it offers us great potential to truly have an impact on ourselves and the people and things we interact with daily.

This chapter provides us with a practical and uplifting system for implementing this path wherever we go, one which can help guide us step by step.

We all know that we live in three dimensions of length, width and height. Now let's expand on this fact and apply it to our topic. Every moment we also live in three other dimensions: the dimensions of the world, of time, and of purpose (23).

The first dimension of world refers to what I call our "package" or our situation in life. It includes the dimensions of all that exists in the world *at this moment*, but more specifically its focus is on us - our immediate and extended families, our jobs, our possessions, our culture, with all its political and socioeconomic aspects. It is also the culmination of everything that has happened to us, the good and the not so good. In other words, it is all that makes us who we are today at this moment in our life journey.

This first dimension requires a basic self-knowledge: awareness and acceptance of who we are and who we are not.

This is our "package." It is hard to improve upon it unless we know our baseline and honestly accept what it is with all its plusses and minuses.

The second dimension is time, which I will refer to as the "process". Time is synonymous with change; life is always in a state of flux. *Without time, change cannot take place. Without change, time has no meaning.* There are always new challenges, opportunities, and people to deal with, and unique problems arise daily.

Each change alters our "package" in some small or large way.

I have done my share of counseling over the years, in many types of situations. The underlying cause of many problems is the difficulty people have in adjusting to changes in their lives (the word *change* is hidden in the word *challenge*). Change can create tension, fear of the unknown, stress, self-doubt, anger, and guilt.

> *We should not look back unless it is to derive useful lessons from past errors and for the purpose of profiting by dearly bought experience.*
> —George Washington

In a life of purpose, though, change is the standard, not the exception. Change is a gift, not an enemy. It is an important ingredient in nudging us into fulfilling our next purpose in life. It pushes us to go with the flow of life and explore the options placed before us. As King Solomon wrote more than 2,800 years ago, "To every time there is a purpose."

The third dimension is "purpose", which underlies the other two. Purpose is a hidden dimension and the driving force that gives meaning to our lives. It is always present in each of our lives but works behind a veil to make room for our free choice. This is the paradox of purpose described earlier.

How do we understand the dimension of purpose in this context?

For some of us, life is incredibly complex and circumstances are constantly changing, largely because of countless choices and decisions we each make every day. There may be multiple purposes working simultaneously in our lives, some even appearing to be contradictory. Sometimes figuring out our purpose and priorities can be as complex as life itself.

For others, depending on lifestyles, surroundings, or personalities, adjustments in our purpose often seem to work slowly. Life-changing events occur only rarely during life, making our unique purpose harder to notice. Life's consistencies and the absence of any challenges can make it difficult to decipher a purpose. Most of us are probably somewhere in between these two extremes.

Purpose is the dimension that explains why our autobiography is ours and no one else's. It provides us with all the tools we need for our journey through life. It is almost like an actual taste of our soul, working from day to day, moment to moment, introducing the tools we need to fulfill our purpose, at the time they are needed.

With these three dimensions in mind, I would like to propose a simple system for you to feel confident in applying purpose to your life. Try the following hat on for size.

At any particular moment, we live at the convergence of these three dimensions. Our Package is passing through the Process of time in order to help us connect to our unique Purpose.

Let's take a moment to absorb that. We are living in our unique package at this unique moment in time. As we go through whatever changes we experience, we realize that in some large or small way these changes can help us fulfill our purpose.

Let's translate this information into our daily lives.

When we face a sudden obstacle or opportunity, we don't avoid or shy away from it; instead it is seen as a potentially important event in today's purpose and we should try to incorporate it into our day. When a request is made of us and we are in the unique position to fulfill it, we realize that quite possibly there is a purpose for why it came to our attention. When an unfortunate event sets us back from reaching a goal, we can see it as part of the hourglass of a bigger development and courageously continue to work toward our goal.

You are the only individual in the world to find yourself, at any moment, at the convergence of these three-dimensional forces in the exact combination in which you are experiencing them. In addition, you have the potential to react to this convergence as no other human being can react.

When we are aware of this convergence *and* we avoid knee-jerk reactions *and* we rise to the occasion with a purposeful response, we are living in 3-P—merging package, process and purpose.

I like to refer to this system as the GPS of purpose, as it helps us get good directions. It adds an additional tool to the map which we created in chapter 6. It helps guide us to fulfill the sixth rung on the purpose ladder.

One of the goals in a life of 3-P is to find the proper balance between the three dimensions. Doing so requires awareness, good judgment, and effort. Each of the three dimensions has a vital role. Ideally they should all work together and help us adjust to changing circumstances. However, we can get out of balance in various ways when aiming to live a life in 3-P.

Some people live solely in the dimension of "package," totally absorbed in the physical world and their attempt to survive, enjoy, and/or control it. Our relationship to the "package" can be very healthy or destructive, or anywhere in between. Many people with unhealthy relationships to their "package" (ranging from addiction to excessive materialism) also have difficulty adjusting to change.

Some people let the dimension of "process" dominate their lives. They may live in the past because they can't rise above a distressful event; others live in the future because of hopes or fears. Others are prisoners of the present, overwhelmed by life or practicing time management to the point of losing touch with how change should affect them.

There are many ways to develop an unhealthy relationship with time. The dimension of time has three stages—past, present, and future. The most important time is the present, because it is there that we live, breathe, love, and struggle. The optimal viewpoint is to balance all three, focusing on the present while building on the past and looking to the future, which makes it possible to attain our fullest potential.

When it comes to the dimension of "purpose," there are also extremes. Some avoid any connection to a sense of "purpose" in life and just live in their "package" and "process." Others are immersed in and driven by the world of "purpose," dedicating their lives to a purpose at the expense of appreciating the dimensions of "package" and "process."[14]

I think it is fair to say that many people today live their lives aiming to balance the dimensions of package and process, but they are not as balanced in the third dimension, the one of purpose. As a result they often can't make sense of life and fall victim to despair when faced with a challenge or when something goes wrong in the other two dimensions.

A structure with only two legs is bound to eventually fall, but a tripod is on solid footing. Similarly, a life without a well-grounded purpose is missing an important dimension. The "package" and the "process" are evolving together to provide us the opportunity to improve something in one or both, as a result of our purpose. If we do not connect with this third dimension, the other two dimensions can cause us to lose our balance.

Every day presents opportunities to merge the three dimensions. Perhaps it is a person who surprisingly comes to us for help, a task we know we need to complete, a coincidence we can't help noticing, or a family member we should devote some time to. It can be an emotion we feel that must be expressed or a dream we must pursue and cannot push off any longer. The details of our life take on new meaning,

---

14 Some gifted individuals have the ability to accomplish much by being totally focused on the dimension of purpose, and for them the other two dimensions can simply be a distraction. We see this with people connected to spiritual/religious endeavors, social action causes, scientific research, academics, etc. Each of these fulfill a purpose path on their own.

especially when these events appear from nowhere or change our routine, and we feel their pull.

Perhaps Viktor E. Frankl said it best in his bestseller *Man's Search for Meaning* when he wrote:

"For the meaning of life differs from man to man, from day to day and from hour to hour. What matters therefore … [is] rather the specific meaning of a person's life at a given moment. To put the question in general terms would be comparable to the question posed to a chess champion: "Tell me, Master, what is the best move in the world?" There simply is no such thing as the best or even a good move apart from a particular situation in a game and the particular personality of one's opponent. The same holds for human existence. .. Everyone has his own specific vocation or mission in life to carry out a concrete assignment which demands fulfillment. Therein he cannot be replaced, nor can his life be repeated. Thus, everyone's task is as unique as is his specific opportunity to implement it. As each situation in life represents a challenge to man and presents a problem for him to solve, the question of the meaning of life may actually be reversed. Ultimately, man should not ask what the meaning of his life is, but rather he must recognize that it is he who is asked. In a word, each man is questioned by life; and he can only answer to life by answering for his own life; to life he can only respond by being responsible". (24)

Life indeed does place us in many situations in which we can either step up to the plate or perhaps miss an opportunity to fulfill a small or large part of our purpose. Hopefully this GPS in a life of purpose will help us identify those opportunities on a regular basis. Living in 3-P will help keep our life well-balanced, and contribute to deepening our connection to purposeful activities on a daily basis.

Thought by thought, word by word, action by action, situation by situation, we can learn how to live a life in 3-P to better bring light into darkness and make the world a better place.

Living a life of purpose, in any or all of the eight paths, should empower us to live in the moment, helping us connect to events in our lives with passion and purpose. When we connect to the full arsenal that a sense of purpose can equip us with, we are better prepared to transform any experience into a positive one.

Let's all take up the challenge to see life as a process of discovering or experiencing our unique purpose and being true to this purpose. Life is about illuminating our inner and outer package with this purpose and constantly growing in our pursuit of it.

As I wrote in the foreword, the thoughts in this book simply reflect my personal filter for the many Jewish and Kabbalistic teachings that are incorporated into my life, combined with my life lessons from the life and death of my dear son. As an aspiring hat maker, I hope and pray that you will be successful in finding a hat here that fits you. I thank you for showing your interest and do hope that you will benefit from this book in some small way, thereby adding to the ripple effect of my son's short but sweet life.

Questions and Exercises

1. Can you accept that your total package today is exactly what it is supposed to be today, and it is the starting point for you to start growing into the rest of your life? Explain.

2. How do you handle changes in your life? Do you try to control time, or do you flow with the process?

3. Do you get stuck or overly attached to events of the past or to your material possessions? Explain.

4. Can you accept that there is a purpose why your body, parents, siblings, children, spouse, friends, neighbors, and business associates are all part of your package? Which part of your package is hard to accept? How can you better accept it?

5. What can you do to better incorporate the dimension of purpose into your life? What obstacles do you have to reaching this goal?

6. Do you think living in 3-P is a goal you can work on? If not, why?

Exercises

1. Next time you experience a surprise person, event, opportunity, or challenge in your life, stop to think what purpose-aligned reaction you should have.

Endnotes

1. Harvard Business Review by George Serafeim and Claudine Gartenberg Oct. 21, 2016

2. Pewresearch.org/fact-tank/2013/09/16/

3. Steven Pinker—Ted.com—April, 2018 (all 6 facts listed)

4. https://www.betterup.co/en-us/about/news-press/press-releases/workers-value-meaning-at-work-new-research-from-betterup-shows-just-how-much-theyre-willing-to-pay-for-it/

5. https://hbr.org/2018/07/creating-a-purpose-driven-organization

6. Givingpledge.org Copyright 2010-2017 - Giving Pledge LLC and its licensors and suppliers

7. Towards a Meaningful Life, HarperCollins, pg. 14

8. Visit www.medicalnewstoday.com/articles/320814.php. Readers are encouraged to do further research into logotherapy.

9. Tanya, Kehot Publications, Chapter 4, pg. 14

10. "He that has silver will not be satisfied with silver ..." (Proverbs 5:9) ("He who has one hundred, desires two hundred ...")

11. Ethics of the Fathers 4:1 ("Who is rich? One who is happy with his lot.")

12. Adapted from Chabad.org/2855443

13. Hayom Yom, Kehot Publications, Elul 3.

14. Talmud Shabbos page 10a —Talmudic commentary on Genesis 2:3

15. Midrash Tanchuma—Portion Bechukosai, sec. 3. This ancient teaching applies to all aspects of our lives and to the world at large. The sages teach us that indeed all mankind is created to fulfill this Higher Purpose, but this purpose is not limited to praying, keeping the Golden Rule, and trying to get as close to God as one can in this lifetime. It is accomplished primarily by carrying out God's will to transform this very imperfect world, and ourselves, through our daily actions. (see A Personal Note on page 158).

16. Public address on Shabbas B'raishis, 1958, para. 9 by Rabbi Menachem Mendel Schneerson, known as "The Lubavitcher Rebbe"—led and transformed the Chabad-Lubavitch Movement into a worldwide presence (1902–1994).

17. Deuteronomy 30:19

18. Likutei Sichos Vol. 28, pg. 82 - Kehot Publications

19. Genesis 1:31

20. Midrash Rabba - Genesis, chapter 9 para. 7: Nahman said in Rabbi Samuel's name: "Behold it was good" refers to the Good Desire; and "Behold, it was very good" to the Evil Desire.

21. Tanya, Kehot Publications, Chap. 6, pg. 20. ("the wicked prevail") by Rabbi Schneur Zalman of Liadi, successor to the Maggid of Mezritch and the founder of the Chabad Chasidic Movement (1745–1812).

22. Talmud Brochot page 54a

23. The Book of Creation 1:5, 44. Attributed to the Patriarch Abraham (1800 BCE–1625 BCE) translated by Arye Kaplan, published by

Sam Weiser, Inc. In Hebrew, these three dimensions are known as olom (world), shana (time), and nefesh (soul). I have taken the liberty (based on commentaries that soul and will are intertwined) to explain this third dimension as purpose, since God's will is for us to fulfill our purpose and the details of creation are driven by that measuring stick, as explained in chapter 4.

24. Man's Search for Meaning by Dr. Viktor E. Frankl,, Pocket Books, 1984 edition, pg. 131. Quote is used to support a life of 3-P, so text was slightly edited. Dr. Frankl is the founder of the Logotherapy school of psychology.

Quotes of famous people are from success.com, goodreads.com, and brainyquote.com

Acknowledgments

I would like to take this opportunity to thank my wife, Chaya, and our children, Mendy, Zalmy, Levi, Moshe, and Chani, for their boundless patience as I spent hundreds of hours working on this book while they were growing up. Their support of this project has been endless. I love them, their wives, and their growing families more than words can express.

I would also like to thank my father, Gerald, and the many friends and colleagues who advised me about the book content over the years, spent hours reading and reacting, and encouraged me in this endeavor. There are too many to list here, but you know who you are, and I do too. I will always be indebted to you for your friendship.

Dedication

*I*t is my special honor to dedicate this book to the three people who have had the greatest influence on my life.

First and foremost, the Lubavitcher Rebbe Menachem Mendel Schneerson of blessed memory, whose life, leadership, and wisdom continue to inspire me in my personal life and my work as his emissary to Long Island.

Secondly, my wife, Chaya, my partner and best friend through all that life has brought us.

And last but not least, our son Boruch Nisan of blessed memory, who came into this world with challenges we never bargained for, but who in his short life touched us profoundly and taught us so much about life, death, and everything in between.

A Personal Note

As the footnotes and endnotes indicate, many of the ideas for this book came from the study of Torah sources and Chabad Chassidic texts. In particular the teachings of my master, teacher, and Rebbe, Rabbi Menachem Mendel Schneerson of blessed memory guided me in my learning and understanding of the many texts that contribute to this book. More about the Rebbe is available on Rebbe.org, and his teachings can be found transposed and explained on Chabad.org as well.

The Torah (the Five Books of Moses, Prophets and Writings, and the Oral Tradition, including Talmud, Chassidic thought/Kabbalah) teaches that the guide for all of mankind to be a partner with God in "fixing" the world was given by God to all of humanity through the Jewish people (together with the responsibility of teaching it to all of humanity) on Mount Sinai more than 3,330 years ago. It includes the explanation of the 613 commandments (279 of which can be fulfilled today) and the almost seventy of which are obligatory to all humanity throughout eternity (known as the Seven Noachide Laws). For a full understanding of these universal laws for all of humanity, visit asknoah. com.

For a better understanding of the ideas in this book or the Torah and its teachings in general, visit your local Chabad center or Chabad.org. A directory of the thousands of Chabad Centers all over the world is found in the right column of the homepage of Chabad.org. Say hello to the rabbi and his wife for me!

This book is meant to be a basic introduction to the topic of purpose. I realize applying purpose to our lives can be a mysterious and complicated matter, and nobody can give an authoritative explanation for all events in our lives. A life of purpose is meant to guide us through life's many challenges in the best way possible.

If enough interest is expressed, I would be happy to address other related issues and questions as best as I can in another book. Feel free to send questions or comments through my website, EightPathsofPurpose. com.

In addition, I do plan on working on a book that will explore the faith path of purpose in greater detail to expand on the wealth of purpose-oriented material connected to belief in a Higher Power.

A Call for Stories

I would also like to compile another book which does require your help. Perhaps you have applied some of the ideas in this book and are just beginning the journey of seeing purpose behind the events of your life. Perhaps you have connected to a warm comfort zone in your depths. It doesn't happen often that events jump out at us with a purposeful meaning, but when they do you usually take note and remember them well.

Sometimes they provide stories that we tell our friends, family, and loved ones. They can be inspiring and meaningful, helping others connect to the events of their lives while looking for that little spark inside themselves. Maybe you found a great way to respond to a challenge in life while incorporating the attitude that there is purpose in everything.

Perhaps it would be good for you to write about how you changed from having a consistent knee-jerk reaction to events to seeing them as having purpose, thus changing the actual results of those events.

I would like to hear from you about any of these stories. They inspire me, and I am sure they will inspire others. In print I hope they can help somebody somewhere find meaning in the events of his or her life. If your story helps just one person or speaks to the heart of a human being in need of that story, you will be adding dimensions to the ripple effect of the event that happened to you and giving it an even deeper purpose to fulfill.

Please send your story to stories@eightpathsofpurpose.com. If enough of you do so, it would make a great book.

Bio

*T*uvia Teldon grew up in Staten Island, NY, graduated high school in St. Louis, Mo., and received his rabbinical ordination from the Central Chabad Rabbinical College in Brooklyn soon after marrying Chaya Leet, who hails from Detroit, Michigan. They moved to Long Island in 1977 to establish the regional headquarters for the International Chabad-Lubavitch Movement and help build the Jewish community.

Rabbi Teldon now serves as the executive director for the thirty-four Chabad centers in Long Island, with a staff of fifty-four full-time rabbis and their wives. He is also rabbi emeritus of the Chabad Jewish Center of Mid-Suffolk and a former member of the East Long Island cabinet for UJA-Federation. He serves on a number of international committees for the worldwide Lubavitch Movement in Brooklyn. He also hosts a weekly interview show on Altice Cable throughout Long Island.

He and his wife Chaya, a well-known global speaker on Jewish topics and a one-time special guest on *The Oprah Show*, live in Commack, Long Island. Their family now consists of five adult children, their spouses, and a growing circle of grandchildren.